WASATCH WINTER TRAILS

WASATCH
WINTER TRAILS

Beginner and Intermediate
Ski and Snowshoe Tours
In the Wasatch and Uinta Mountains

BY JOHN VERANTH

Editor\   Martha Morrison Veranth

Cover\   Easton Design

Reviewers\   Milton Hollander
                  Norman Fish
                  Bruce Tremper

Production\   David Berger

Copyright ©1991 Wasatch Publishers

Wasatch Publishers
4460 Ashford Drive
Salt Lake City, Utah 84124

Library of Congress Catalog Number: 91–066689
ISBN Number 0-915272-36-9

Disclaimer

Personal Responsibility

Winter travel in the mountains is hazardous. A guidebook is not a substitute for individual training and judgment. Every skier is personally responsible for obtaining proper instruction in ski technique and winter safety and for carrying adequate food, clothing, and emergency gear. Evaluate the weather, the snow conditions, and the physical condition of everyone in your group before deciding to do a specific tour.

Avalanche

The route, slope angle, and avalanche path data was collected from various sources as an aid in trip planning. Known risk areas are identified but the absence of marked risks does not guarantee safety. Pockets of unstable snow that are too small to map can bury a skier. Unusual weather can cause normally stable areas to avalanche. Do not venture beyond your ability to understand and evaluate conditions on the ground.

Contents

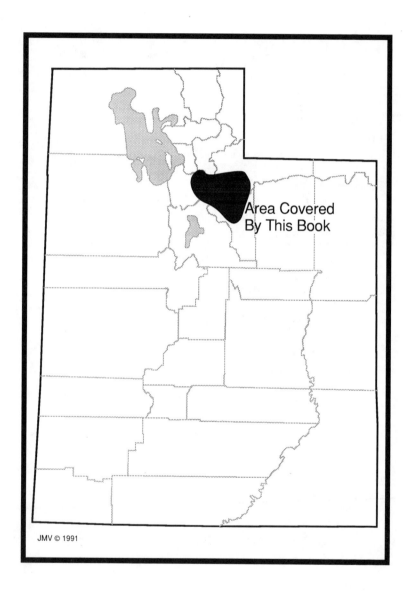

Area Covered
By This Book

JMV © 1991

List of Maps

A winter morning at Dog Lake Flats above Brighton

Introduction

Here is a guide to some of the beginner and intermediate difficulty winter trails that are available to ski tourers and snowshoers. The trails are all readily accessible from the cities along the Wasatch Front and offer outstanding winter recreation.

The selected trails are in popular areas with little dangerous terrain, an important consideration for the first few seasons. This is not a comprehensive guidebook and many more areas, especially in the Uinta foothills, are available to those who want to explore.

Winter backcountry travel by ski and by snowshoe is the focus of this guidebook. Track skiing and lift-assisted skiing are discussed mainly as a way to develop skills for backcountry tours. The advanced routes onto the high ridges and summits of the Wasatch and long-distance routes in the Uintas are not included since this is a guide for casual tourers. The main ski mountaineering routes have been mapped and documented in other sources. This book was compiled to direct new skiers to already popular areas and to help experienced skiers find new tours.

The essential information that every skier should know is reviewed but this is a trail guidebook, not a self-teaching manual. Suggestions for formal instruction and further reading are provided.

Climbing up for another delightful run in Powder Park.

1

WINTER TRAILS

Weather, geography, and human activity define and constrain the winter trails in the Wasatch and Uinta mountains. Utah is a desert and precipitation is greatest where the clouds pass over mountain summits. The Wasatch Fault is one of the world's major escarpments while the Uintas are a broad uplift surrounded by a piedmont. Both ranges have been heavily glaciated at higher elevations.

As a result, the canyons along the Wasatch front are steep and have high avalanche danger at upper elevations while the Wasatch back and Uinta foothills are at a similar elevation but are more gentle. Tours in the Wasatch are uphill and downhill. Tours in the Uintas are more gradual but distances are far longer.

Backcountry skiers and downhill skiers compete for the same terrain: the gentle bowls at the heads of the canyons.

The Wasatch is right next to the urban centers but most of the gentle terrain is in downhill areas. Downhill skiing is big business and snow plowing for skier parking costs money. The Uinta foothills have excellent backcountry terrain but few access roads and fewer designated skier parking areas. These factors were all considered in selecting the routes to describe in this book.

Seasons and Snow Conditions

When selecting a place to ski on a given day you need to consider the season, the minimum and maximum elevation of the planned route, and the predominant direction that the slope faces (usually called the slope aspect).

The backcountry ski season usually starts with the first heavy snowstorm in November and ends when everyone gets tired of skiing in the spring. Midwinter often has an extended period of high avalanche danger throughout the area. This is caused by weak snow layers at the bottom of the snowpack and the heavy new accumulation above. This is also the time of cold, storms, and short days. The best skiing is often in February and early March when the snowpack has consolidated, avalanche danger is low, the snow is deep, and days are warm.

In the Wasatch, the following elevation generalizations are useful:

5000 to 7500 feet — Snowfall is limited and the snow melts quickly, so the skiing is good only in midwinter or right after a major storm. Slopes are gentle and avalanche danger is low.

7500 to 9000 feet — This is where the best beginner to intermediate skiing is found. The snowfall is heavier and the good powder lasts longer.

9000 feet to summits — The heavy snowfall and the steep slopes near the ridge crests make superb skiing but the only intermediate skiing at this elevation is in the side canyon bottoms and in the bowls at the heads of the canyons. Most other areas are advanced to expert terrain. Some areas are scraped bare and other areas have extreme avalanche danger due to wind redeposition of snow.

The slope aspect controls how much wind and sunlight reach the snow. North-facing slopes have the best powder skiing but also have the greatest avalanche danger. South-facing slopes are warm and sunny and have fewer trees, which makes for pleasant touring. But the intense sun on south-facing slopes means that snow goes from powder to crust to cement much faster. East- and west-facing slopes are intermediate between these extremes and are most affected by the prevailing winds.

The wonderful thing about Utah is the variety caused by elevation and terrain differences. Whatever the season or weather there is always somewhere to go to enjoy a winter trail.

Types of Winter Trails

Winter snow travel has evolved into several overlapping sports. Each has distinct equipment and objectives but there is enough overlap that most enthusiasts enjoy more than one.

Backcountry skiing is winter hiking. Today, backcountry touring remains the closest to skiing's roots as a way to travel during the long northern European winters. The emphasis is on viewing the scenery, getting exercise, and enjoying the social experience (which can include simple solitude). It is a form of skiing that can be done nearly anywhere there is snow. But in the Wasatch there is little of the "classic nordic" terrain associated with cross-country skiing in Scandinavia or the midwest. The Uintas offer large areas for nordic skiing but much of the Wasatch is ski mountaineering terrain.

Snowshoes are an alternative form of winter hiking. They are easier to master than skis but require more energy to travel any distance. Snowshoes excel for winter wildlife viewing because they offer a stable footing.

15

Track skiing is a specialized form of touring that uses very lightweight equipment. The emphasis is on aerobic exercise, speed, form and style. Track skiing is winter jogging (a wax company actually trademarked the term ski jogging ®) and is done on the groomed areas listed in the fee section.

Lift-assisted skiing on backcountry equipment starts as a way to practice skiing many hills in one day. For some it evolves into an alternative style of downhill skiing with the added challenge of having a loose heel and the incredible satisfaction of carving graceful telemark turns down through the moguls.

Ski mountaineering is winter mountain climbing and appeals to the brave and strong. The goal is the spectacular destination, the triumph of a summit or ridge crest, and the thrill of the long downhill drop over untracked slopes.

Definitions

Going from beginner to expert terrain, slopes become steeper, the snow becomes more variable, trails become narrower, and rocks and trees become more prominent. For the purposes of describing skill levels and trail difficulty this book uses the following terms:

Novice: A person on skis (or snowshoes) for the first few times. Novices have problems with balance, maneuvering, and endurance.

Beginner: A person who is comfortable on gentle terrain. Beginners can descend hills by using a snowplow to come to a stop then doing a kick turn.

Intermediate: A person who can control speed and can turn on low angle hills with good snow conditions and who has good technique for covering distance without getting exhausted. Intermediate skiers should be able to ski the "Easiest" runs at a downhill ski area making linked turns without falling.

Advanced: A person who can turn on open hills under mixed snow conditions and who can survival ski down steep chutes and through thick trees. Advanced skiers should have had formal instruction in avalanche safety and should enjoy skiing the "More Difficult" downhill runs on backcountry skis.

Expert: You recognize them by the graceful tracks down the steepest slopes.

The words "easy" and "difficult" will be used in the context of the overall route description. A "difficult hill" on a tour described as suitable for beginners will be objectively easier than an "easy descent" on a route described as suitable for advanced skiers.

Canyon Transportation

Getting from home to the trailhead is part of every tour. Driving canyon roads and finding a plowed place to park are winter challenges. Although the distances are longer, access to the trails on the back of the Wasatch is often easier than getting to trails in the tri-canyon area.

Driving

The canyon roads are steep and receive heavy snowfall, and some cross serious avalanche danger zones. Snow tires or chains are required in Big and Little Cottonwood Canyons during the winter and are highly recommended for all other mountain roads as well. Proper traction is important for your own safety and to avoid causing traffic jams on the hills. Being trapped behind a car that could not climb from the Alta parking lot to the highway was a common situation before these rules were instituted. The snow tire rule is often enforced by a sheriff's roadblock at the mouth of the canyon, especially during storms.

Roads on the back side of the Wasatch and the Uinta foothills are generally plowed as far as the last tax-paying residence or to a designated snowmobile parking area. For many tours, this means walking or skiing several miles along an unplowed road before getting to the really good skiing.

Parking

Parking is limited to plowed turnouts and lots. Park carefully in the available space to leave room for others. Observe "No Parking" signs and never leave your car with two wheels on the paved portion of the road. Always meet your friends in the valley and carpool up the canyons.

In the Wasatch, there is limited canyon-bottom space and the Salt Lake County canyon master plan limits future expansion of parking. The community consensus was that we should not "pave paradise and turn it into a parking lot." Backcountry skier parking has been tolerated in most downhill area parking lots but resorts would rather have the space for lift ticket customers. We all need to cooperate to use available parking efficiently.

Skier parking behind the Wasatch ranges from excellent along the Beaver Creek trail to non-existent at Daniels Pass. Improved access and parking will open many more areas to casual touring.

Bus System

The Ski Bus operated by the Utah Transit Authority is an alternative that is environmentally sound, economical, and reasonably convenient. The buses have several pickup points in the valley and go to the developed ski areas. The Spruces Trailhead in Big Cottonwood and the White Pine Trailhead in Little Cottonwood are also designated stops. The ski bus is especially useful in planning inter-canyon tours. Call 287-4636 for current route schedules.

Watershed Sanitation

The Wasatch Front canyons have been managed as watershed since the 1920's and this is still the dominant management priority. The Wasatch National Forest was established largely to protect the watershed and Salt Lake City has acquired most of the land north of Parleys Canyon for watershed. Little Cottonwood, Big Cottonwood, City Creek and Parleys Canyons are the main water source for Salt Lake City. The Provo River in the Uintas flows into Deer Creek Reservoir - a major water source for Salt Lake and Utah counties. Protect your drinking water.

Winter users need to be especially aware of watershed sanitation since "digging a hole 6 inches into the soil" is not possible under four feet of snow. The Salt Lake City Water Department and the Forest Service have placed toilets at many popular trailheads. Use them! Because of the effort and the cold, ski tours tend to be much shorter than summer hikes. There is no excuse for having to defecate during a 3- or 4-hour tour. Health considerations caused Mount Rainier National Park to institute a pack-it-out policy for overnight climbers on the high glaciers. That is something to consider for the heavily used Wasatch.

Remember — leave nothing in the snow that you would not want to drink.

Guidebooks & Maps - Cautions

No guidebook is a substitute for good judgment. Use the information in this book to plan your trips but observe and think for yourself before starting on a tour.

The maps in this book are at a reduced scale and are intended to supplement information in the winter trail descriptions. Full-scale USGS topographic maps should be used for planning any off-trail or advanced routes.

The areas where slopes are above 30° are shaded for quick reference but every skier should know how to check slope angle on maps and on the ground. A slope angle gage is printed on the back cover of this book. By comparing the spacing of lines on the topographic map to the gage you can determine the approximate slope along your route. Be aware that a slope too short to appear on a topographic map can still avalanche.

Estimating slope angle on the ground takes practice. Several inclinometers suitable for backcountry use are available in ski shops. Use an inclinometer until you develop a "calibrated eyeball."

Winter routes are not as precisely defined as summer trails. The exact length of the route depends on how many switchbacks you make, so a skier with waxed skis will travel farther than someone using climbing skins. The energy expended depends on the snow conditions and these change from day to day. Ascent and descent routes are often different. Ascent routes are selected for easy climbing and avoiding avalanche paths while descent routes follow the steeper, more open slopes.

For these reasons the mileages given in the tour descriptions are the approximate canyon-bottom distances from trailhead to destination. Backcountry distances are rounded to the nearest quarter mile. In a route description, the term "immediately" means a very short distance, typically within sight or less than a couple of minutes of skiing.

Time estimates for winter tours are not accurate because snow conditions change. To be conservative in trip planning, assume less than one mile per hour for a small party breaking trail through fresh snow. Estimate ascents at no more than 1000 vertical feet per hour even when following a broken track.

The words "left" and "right" are for travel in the direction of the route description. Most descriptions are written for travel in the uphill direction, so referring to "the left side of the stream" is the reverse of the usual geographic convention.

Routefinding

Getting to the trailhead is often the hardest part of routefinding on a tour, so special care was given to trailhead descriptions. Signs are useful but they are often missing due to agency budget cuts or malicious vandalism. The trailheads are described in terms of mileages from major road intersections or similar landmarks. Road mileages given as decimal fractions were determined by odometer readings.

Following someone's tracks is the most common routefinding technique for beginner and intermediate skiers in the backcountry. The routes described here are all popular tours and you will rarely be the first on the tour after a snowstorm. When following tracks you still need to navigate. Be aware of junctions where some skiers may have gone up a different side drainage than the route to your destination. A set of tracks across a known avalanche path is not an unconditional guarantee of safety.

If you stick to popular tours during good weather you can get by with rudimentary routefinding skills. But wind and drifting snow can obliterate a track within hours. Also, there are times when you may be first on the route after a storm. Get in the habit of following your route on a map so you learn how to relate the map to what you see on the ground. Look around on the ascent and remember landmarks.

Fresh snow with no tracks should be an opportunity for powder skiing, not an intimidating routefinding experience. If you can use map and compass to find your way in summer, the same skills will work in winter.

The fee tracks are an excellent place to practice when you are just learning to ski.

2

LEARNING TO SKI
THE WASATCH
BACKCOUNTRY

The mountains are especially beautiful and inviting in winter, but they are also intimidating, especially for the first-time skier. This chapter outlines the things you will need to learn and suggests places to go for instruction and practice. The essentials of technique and safety are discussed for review and for the benefit of those who have skied in other areas but are not familiar with local conditions.

This is a description of places, not a self-teaching manual. Learning to execute linked telemark turns, or learning to evaluate a snow pit for avalanche risk are skills best learned from personal instruction.

Instruction and Practice

If you are just starting to ski, this is what I recommend for the first season. Start with one or two lessons at a fee track. These commercial operations offer group and private lessons that can be tailored to your pace and ability. Learning technique from an expert is much more productive than trying to learn on your own and gets you off to a good start. Between lessons, practice on your own on a fee track or on a flat undeveloped area. Excellent novice practice areas are at Mountain Dell or the flat areas near the White Pine and Beaver Creek trailheads.

Once you feel confident moving around, try a couple of the shorter and flatter beginner tours such as the Mill Creek road, the Spruces Campground, or a short section of the Beaver Creek trail. These all are easy routes to follow and tours of different lengths are possible.

After mastering the stop and kick turn technique, you can progress to some more interesting terrain such as Willow Lake or Albion Basin, Yellow Pine, or Daniels Pass. These tours are fun and give you the chance to do some routefinding and to practice on hills.

Mastering hills is the most difficult step for the first season. You get some practice on short hills on beginner tours but you really do not get enough practice in a day to improve quickly. Skiing the beginner slope at a downhill area is the best way to get practice on hills quickly.

When doing lift-assisted skiing there are several precautions. The downhill areas require safety straps to keep your skis attached if a binding separates. If you are using waxed skis, be sure your wax is not too soft (sticky) for the snow conditions. Being unable to slide as you get off the chairlift at the top is dangerous. Also, avoid wearing a large pack on the chairlift as it gets in the way. If you are unfamiliar with chair lifts, ask the attendant for instruction or plan to start with a "hills on pin bindings" lesson.

Return to the lift areas occasionally until you can turn consistently, then try some of the intermediate tours listed in this book. Catherine Pass from Brighton, Dog Lake, and White Pine are good tours at this stage.

Avalanche awareness is important to your own safety and to the safety of your companions. Plan to take an avalanche safety course before you start skiing in areas where there is significant risk.

Survival Skiing Techniques on Descent

Staying in control while going downhill is often harder than the climb. Executing perfect linked turns straight down the hill requires timing, balance, moderate strength, and lots of practice. Beginning and intermediate skiers are often confronted with the problem of just getting down a short but (to them) steep section of trail. Every backcountry skier is occasionally confronted with the problem of safely getting down a slope that is steeper, icier, or narrower than expected, making it too difficult to execute controlled turns. Crashing and falling repeatedly is time-consuming and physically exhausting. Intimidating descents, where the only route is walled by rocks and trees, keep many new tourers out of some of the best places.

There are many "survival skiing" techniques that are not elegant but will get you down without becoming injured or exhausted.

Snowshoes are one solution. Snowshoes are much easier to master and allow even beginners to travel into rugged areas in winter.

Another solution, especially when the snow is packed to ice, is to simply take your skis off and walk the difficult section. Tie the skis to your pack and use your ski poles for balance. Walking is no disgrace and will often save time in the end.

Descending by traversing across the hill, coming to a complete stop, then making a kick turn and traversing in the opposite direction is the way most skiers deal with slopes beyond their ability. This is slow but it will get you down. Practice kick turns on short hills so you are comfortable with the feeling.

Narrow trails and chutes can be handled by skiing in a very aggressive snowplow or by side-slipping using the ski edges for control. This technique demands a lot of leg effort, so stop and relax your legs periodically. Keep your speed down by frequently coming to a stop. If you speed up out of control, sit down in a controlled manner that keeps your legs straight downhill. Getting back up from this position is easier than pulling yourself together after a "head plant" or an arms-and-legs-flailing fall.

Using these techniques will allow you to visit more interesting areas and to push yourself. After a while you will find that you are enjoying smooth turns down slopes that you originally had to survival ski.

Ski Equipment

When buying equipment you need to tell the seller what type of skiing you will be doing most often. Many beginners buy "golf course skis" suitable only for tracks and gentle terrain and are then disappointed when they try to ski the typical Wasatch backcountry. Fortunately, most of the ski specialist shops rent equipment and some will credit a portion of the rental toward a purchase. This allows you to try different types of skis and boots and get a first-hand idea of the differences.

Steep slopes can be safely descended by coming to a complete stop and then doing a kick turn.

The wax, fishscale, or skins question can be answered by saying that they all have a place. Non-slip ski bottom patterns work moderately well under a wide range of snow conditions and far surpass waxed skis in the spring when there is powder in the trees and slush in the sunshine. Most waxless skis do not have an aggressive enough pattern to handle the steeper Wasatch tours but wax can be applied over fishscale patterns for extra grip.

Wax gives the ability to fine-tune the ski to the snow conditions and is the choice for people who enjoy experimenting and fiddling with equipment. Computer hackers and drivers of manual shift cars are good candidates for waxed skis. Because the Wasatch is steep, I normally wax to obtain extra grip at the expense of glide. This means using about one wax grade softer than the manufacturer's charts recommend. Unfortunately, there are many days in the Wasatch where wax does not have enough grip to climb the trails unless you go to the "bubble-gum" soft waxes and messy klisters.

If you want to do the intermediate difficulty backcountry tours listed in this book and plan to eventually do advanced tours, get a ski that performs on varied terrain and buy climbing skins. My recommendation is to select a metal edge ski optimized for backcountry turns. Stiffness, side-cut, and camber are technical terms for some features that the manufacturer controls to obtain a specific performance. New and better models come out each year and the specialist shops can direct you to the backcountry models. Climbing skins are strap-on or self-sticking strips of synthetic fur or snake-skin pattern plastic that give the best possible traction on the ascent. At the mountain top or turnaround point you remove the skins and apply a hard ski wax to get just the right degree of glide and control on the downhill. The metal edge adds weight but greatly increases the ability to slow down, turn, and stop on hard snow.

ESSENTIALS

Travel in the winter backcountry requires the proper equipment to take care of yourself under reasonably foreseeable circumstances.

The ESSENTIALS include:

Layered clothes — A cool ventilating layer, a wind protection layer, and a warm layer.

Extra clothes in the pack.

Hat and gloves or mittens.

Sun protection — Sunglasses, a sunblock lotion, and lip protection.

Food, water, and possibly a hot drink.

Map and compass.

First aid supplies.

Duct tape for emergency repairs.

For Lift Assisted Tours:

Ski retainer straps (mandatory on ski lifts).

A very small pack.

As you begin to do more tours in areas with avalanche risk each member of the party should carry:

Shovel, sturdy enough to dig hard snow.

Avalanche transponder.

Grizzly Gulch Trail: Although this is a beginner route, the sidehills are steep and have known avalanche paths. Be aware of the snow stability on the aspects you will be skiing across and below.

3

WINTER SAFETY

Weather and avalanche are winter killers. Be very cautious on tours until you gain knowledge through reading, formal training, contact with more experienced skiers, and personal experience. The best way to learn is to observe conditions on the winter trails and compare your observations to what you have been taught.

Weather

Air gets colder with altitude and winds are higher near ridges and summits, so the wind chill on a ski tour can be severe. Wind chill temperature combines actual air temperature with wind speed to give a single measure of the rate of heat loss from bare skin. Conditions where bare skin will freeze within minutes are possible in the Wasatch. Protection for the nose, ears, and fingers is especially important.

Hypothermia is a general drop in body temperature due to prolonged exposure to cold, wet conditions. More hypothermia cases occur when temperatures are near freezing than when it is extremely cold. This is a very dangerous condition since the early symptoms of hypothermia include lethargy, mental confusion and loss of coordination. Since victims quickly loose the ability to help themselves it is important for everyone in a group to watch for the danger signs in the others.

Prevent hypothermia by staying warm and dry. Remove clothing layers to keep from sweating on the uphill sections and have some extra warm layers in the pack to put on quickly when you stop.

Whiteout is a condition where low clouds and blowing snow make the earth and sky merge into a blur with no defined horizon or distant landmarks. Watch from the valley and notice how often the Wasatch summits are in the clouds during winter storms and you will understand that whiteout is common. One danger is getting totally lost, especially when skiing near ridges where you can descend into the wrong drainage. Another danger is that you lose all sense of the distance and angle of the slope. Avoid skiing into poor visibility conditions and watch for storms moving in your direction. Once you gain experience, a map, a compass, and a good memory of the terrain will allow you to risk skiing in a whiteout.

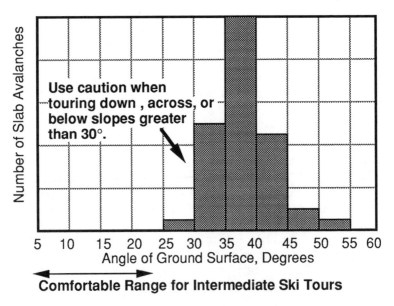

Data: Avalanche Handbook, US Forest Service

Avalanche

Avalanches are a serious danger and backcountry travelers must plan their tours to avoid times and places of high risk. The steep slopes in the Wasatch have very high avalanche risk and there have been many avalanche fatalities. Planning the tour to avoid unstable snow is vital because the statistics are grim.

Studies show that 95% of avalanche accidents are triggered by the victim. About a third of the avalanche victims are killed by trauma and are dead when the snow stops moving. Once buried, a surviving skier has less than 30 minutes to live under the snow.

Avoidance is the only safe course. Avalanche search and rescue is uncertain and often becomes body recovery. Beginners need to be extremely cautious. An expert's tracks down a headwall slope look impressive but safely skiing this terrain requires a complete understanding of how slope angle, aspect, recent weather, and snowpack layers affect stability at that precise time and that specific location. Prudent skiers will avoid all potentially hazardous terrain until they develop good avalanche evaluation skills.

The routes selected for this book avoid the most hazardous terrain but the Wasatch is so steep that nearly all routes cross areas that slide at least occasionally. Skier judgment is needed. All skiers, including beginners, need to recognize a few basic factors that affect avalanche risk.

Slope — Most avalanche releases occur on slopes between 30 and 45 degrees. Lower angle slopes hold the snow until it melts and steeper slopes slide continuously as the snow falls.

Recent Weather — Most avalanches occur during or soon after storms. A snowfall rate greater than one inch per hour indicates a rapidly increasing risk. Periods of high wind move snow around, increasing risk on the lee slopes. Another high risk time is around mid-morning to early afternoon in late spring when the old snow warms up and the surface layers begin to slide.

Snowpack History — Most years, a weak layer called "depth hoar" or "temperature gradient snow" or "faceted snow" forms near the ground. When this happens the avalanche hazard will remain high for weeks until the snow finally consolidates or until major avalanches that run to the ground scour away the weak layer. Warm and cold cycles can leave weak layers in the middle of the snowpack as well. The Avalanche Forecast Center recording always includes a discussion of the layering in the snowpack, so listening to the recording on a regular basis provides a good education.

Aspect — After a windstorm, the lee slopes have a higher risk than windward slopes. Sunny slopes consolidate faster in winter but are less stable in warm spring weather. In the Wasatch and Uintas these factors mean that north and east slopes generally have greater risk in winter. West and south facing slopes generally have greater risk in spring.

There are exceptions and elaborations that apply to all these statements but the wise tourer will err on the side of caution.

Avoiding Avalanches

The best route selection is to travel only in areas with the elevation, slope angle, and aspect known to have a low avalanche hazard on that day.

Watch the slope angle. Plan your trips to avoid travel on slopes with an angle over 30° until you have developed good avalanche evaluation skills.

Call the Utah Avalanche Forecast Center recording and listen carefully for the safe aspects and elevations on the day you plan to ski.

Observe conditions along your route. If you see suspicious signs, be cautious and collect all available information. Turn back if you are in doubt about the snow stability.

Trip Planning

The maps in this book show information to aid in route selection. Slopes between 30 and 50 degrees are marked with a shading pattern. This is the area where most avalanches release so skill in route selection and an understanding of snow stability are essential for any party that skis down, across, or below these areas. In the central Wasatch, known avalanche paths that cross or are near a marked route are also shown. This avalanche path mapping was compiled from published sources and is an aid in route planning. The fact that an area is not shown as an avalanche path is no guarantee of safety. Many ava-

Avalanche debris melting in spring at the Red Pine trail junction. Unusual weather can cause normally stable areas to slide.

lanches, once released, run out onto the low angle flats below, and unusual weather can cause nearly any area to slide.

Comparing the avalanche paths with slope angles illustrates an important principle. Most avalanches release on slopes over 30° but not all slopes over 30° are avalanche paths. Some slopes are stable because the snowpack is well anchored to the ground by terrain or by thick trees. Safe routes and times exist but you have to know where and when to find them.

The maps in this book, combined with the full-scale USGS topographic maps, show the information needed to judge slope angle, aspect, and elevation of your proposed route.

Most skiers are caught in human-released avalanches rather than in naturally released avalanches that descend on them from above. The time of greatest risk is when someone is on the slope. Plan ascents to avoid having the entire party directly below the lead skier and when possible cross suspicious areas one at a time.

Utah Avalanche Forecast Center

The Utah Avalanche Forecast Center is an important resource for all backcountry users. The highly experienced staff monitors snow reports throughout the winter and prepares a daily report that is available over the telephone.

Call the forecast center recording before venturing out. Listen carefully and take notes. Usually there is a discussion of the recent weather and snow conditions followed by evaluations of hazard conditions. A typical statement in the forecast might be *"Moderate hazard on north and east facing slopes greater than 35 degrees and above 9000 feet."* Listen for the qualifying statements and not just for the simple "high" or "low" words.

Use the topographic map to determine the elevation, slope angle, and aspect along your route. Compare this to the information from the Avalanche Forecast Center to decide if your planned route is entering potentially unstable areas. When avalanche danger along your intended route is high due to recent weather, ski on lower angle slopes and on different aspects, or go another day. Do not travel into deadly situations.

PHONE NUMBERS

The Utah Avalanche Forecast Center provides an updated recorded message by 7:30 every morning and the recording is often updated in the afternoon as well. Since a storm that hits Logan may miss Provo, separate recordings are prepared for each region along the Wasatch. Due to inadequate field reports, forecasts are not prepared specifically for the Uintas, but the Park City area forecast provides some information.

Logan Mountains **752-4146**	Includes the Bear River and Wellsville ranges. Extends from the Utah-Idaho border to Sardine Canyon.
Ogden Mountains **621-2362**	Includes the Wasatch from Sardine Canyon in the north to City Creek Canyon in the south.
Salt Lake Mountains **364-1581**	Includes from City Creek to Box Elder Peak. Primarily covers the Millcreek, Big Cottonwood, Little Cottonwood area.
Provo Mountains **374-9770**	Covers from Box Elder Peak to Mt Nebo and east to Daniels Canyon.
Park City Mountains **649-2250**	The back side of the Wasatch from Lambs Canyon to Snake Creek. Occasional information from the Uintas.

Field Evaluation

Avalanche is a natural winter process that occurs whenever the weight of new snow exceeds the strength of the underlying snow layers. If you want to ski near or in areas that have a moderate avalanche hazard, you need to know how to find the safe path and how to avoid the danger areas.

Experienced skiers plan their routes to stay on the safer aspects whenever possible and use the protection of minor ridges and other terrain features. Doing field evaluations that combine digging snow pits with other observations is important. Snow stability changes with elevation and aspect, and risk can be very different on opposite sides of the ridge separating two canyons even when the horizontal distance is less than a mile, or in extreme cases only a few yards across the crest.

After setting out on a tour, observe conditions along your route. Look for signs of recent avalanche activity. Be cautious if there has been recent rapid loading of either new snow or wind deposited snow onto the existing snowpack. Sounds of collapsing or cracking are an indicator of weakness in the snowpack. Digging a snowpit and inspecting the layers provides slope-specific information about the history of the snowpack.

Evaluating avalanche hazard on a backcountry slope and finding the safest route through high-risk terrain require specialized study. Books alone are not enough. Taking professionally-taught courses that include field work sessions is essential for anyone who aspires to ski the steep and deep powder runs.

HAZARD WORDS

Single words oversimplify statements about avalanche risk. When listening to the Utah Avalanche Forecast Center recording, pay attention to the qualifying statements about slope angle, aspect and elevation. Since the hazard level words are used in the forecasts, knowing the accepted definitions of these words is important.

LOW: Mostly stable snow exists, except in isolated pockets. Human-triggered avalanches, except small slides, are unlikely. Explosives or large falling cornices may release slides.

MODERATE: Localized areas of unstable snow exist. Human-triggered avalanches are possible and may be dangerous.

HIGH: Widespread areas of unstable snow exist. Human-triggered avalanches are likely, and natural or spontaneous avalanches are possible.

EXTREME: Widespread areas of unstable snow exist. Human-triggered avalanches are certain and large, destructive natural avalanches are possible.

Avalanche Safety Instruction

Short avalanche awareness courses are offered free or at minimum cost but cover only the basics that **everyone** should know even when following behind a more experienced skier.

The most exciting backcountry skiing is in the same areas that have slopes steep enough to be dangerous. If you want to learn to ski these areas take a professionally-taught avalanche course first.

Several commercial courses designed for the recreational skier are taught in Utah each year. The courses are advertised through posters in the ski shops, and listings appear in the Sierra Club and Wasatch Mountain Club newsletters. The Utah Avalanche Forecast Center office also provides information on available courses. A typical course will cover the types of mountain weather, the process of recrystallization and consolidation in the snow pack, field stability evaluation, route selection, and search and rescue in great detail.

There is a lot of material to cover and these courses require several days of classroom and field sessions. The texts and handouts for a typical course are over 400 pages. That is one reason why this book does not attempt to even summarize stability evaluation.

Search and Rescue

An organized rescue party has almost no chance of accomplishing a live recovery. Getting help in a backcountry emergency will require several hours but 50% of buried skiers die of suffocation within 30 minutes. The others in the party are the only resource that can save a buried companion.

Although the intention is to avoid getting caught in an avalanche, everyone skiing known risk areas should carry a large, sturdy shovel, an electronic avalanche transmitter and receiver beacon (Pieps ®), and other emergency gear. Avalanche beacons are the only reliable way a small party can search and dig out a buried companion in time. This gear will do no good unless you learn to use it and practice avalanche search several times each season. Having current advanced first aid and CPR training is also important.

This may all sound very grim but the danger is real. In recent years increased public awareness of avalanche hazards has been an important factor in improving winter safety. Even though there are more skiers in the Wasatch than before, there have been fewer backcountry fatalities. The winter backcountry is a magnificent place but requires knowledge to be safe. There are many low-risk areas for casual tourers to enjoy. Developing the knowledge and skill needed to safely ski the more spectacular areas requires a major commitment.

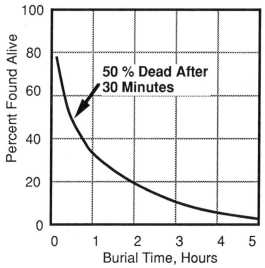

Data: Avalanche Handbook, US Forest Service

Touring above the Brighton lifts. Backcountry and downhill skiers compete for the same terrain — the gentle bowls at the heads of the canyons.

4

LAND MANAGEMENT

The backcountry ski experiences that we enjoy today are the cumulative result of land management decisions made over a period of decades. Everyone who enjoys the splendor of natural places needs to be an advocate for the protection of these areas.

Why We Lost The Good Beginner Touring

Finding good beginner routes for this book was not easy. Of the nine beginner tours listed in Alexis Kelner's 1976 guidebook *Wasatch Tours*, only four remain in this book. Three were lost to downhill ski runs, one has become a fee area, and one is on private land and the road is now being used more heavily by residents. But only three of 27 intermediate tours were lost to downhill ski areas and none of the advanced and super-tours have been affected.

The problem is that during the initial round of forest plans prepared in the 1970's the heads of the canyons were identified as areas to be managed for "developed recreation" while the areas downcanyon were identified for "dispersed recreation." Also, mining history left large blocks of private land mixed with the Forest Service land.

The result was that the downhill ski areas got nearly all the high elevation, gentle terrain in the Wasatch. Most of the "dispersed recreation" area is so steep and has such high avalanche risk that it is suitable only for ski mountaineering, not for casual touring.

The Ski Interconnect and the Olympics are two forces that could most change the Wasatch. An interconnect will adversely affect summer and winter backcountry users because "interconnecting" the developed ski areas will "disconnect" existing backcountry areas with strips of downhill-managed areas. The issue is not simply the loss of a few acres of backcountry. Customer safety and liability issues will require the interconnected resorts to manage the interconnect runs with ski patrol and avalanche control activity. Tours that backcountry users have been doing for decades will be severed by "Area Closed" signs that have the force of law.

The promise of the Olympic promoters not to propose venues in Big and Little Cottonwood Canyons has been matched by local environmental groups agreeing not to oppose the Olympic bid. Yet the fame resulting from the Olympic bid will bring more development pressure on these sensitive mountains.

Ultimately, there is the issue of how much development is appropriate for the Wasatch. The swaths cut for winter ski runs, the lift access roads, and the lift structures themselves drastically affect the experience of both hikers and motorized sightseers in summer. Wildlife, watershed, and the simple protection of a few remaining natural places are issues that need consideration.

Plowing and Parking

Conveniently located trailhead parking is necessary for reaching backcountry areas. Parking on the shoulder of roads hampers snow removal, is a traffic hazard, and is illegal on main roads. Plowing winter trailheads costs money. Snowmobilers have a program where a portion of their vehicle registration fee goes into a fund for plowing parking areas, so there are many well-located snowmachine trailheads. Other states have legislated a winter recreation parking sticker program for muscle-powered sports. Utahns still need to address this issue.

Citizen Action

The Salt Lake County Master Plan was hammered out over a period of several years with intense citizen participation. The general guidance of the document is preservation of the canyons in a natural state consistent with existing property rights and public safety needs. Environmental groups' representatives worked hundreds of hours on the Citizen Advisory Committee. The public hearings were packed with concerned citizens, questionnaires were diligently filled out, and many letters were written to the planning staff and to the County Commission.

There will be more battles that will require similar effort if we are to protect our natural places. Another round of forest plans is due in the next decade and citizens need to emphasize the protection and preservation role of the Forest Service to offset the promoters of development and resource extraction. The canyon master plan will not protect the canyons unless citizens exert pressure against approving variances. Every ski area is likely to want to expand beyond its existing boundaries.

The Uinta foothills are the future of backcountry skiing in Utah. The Forest Service, the Highway Department, and the county governments need to update their plans to accommodate this increased and changing use.

If you care about these issues, get involved. Attend hearings and write letters when an issue comes up for public comment. A strong expression of citizen concern will influence policy makers.

The groomed tracks are popular with serious racers, Lycra-clad ski-skaters, and casual skiers who like the predictability of a marked and maintained course.

5

FEE AREAS

Ski touring venues range from nicely groomed tracks to wilderness backcountry. This chapter covers the commercially-operated fee areas in the central Wasatch. The next chapter covers several designated ski areas that offer fewer amenities but are available without charge. The last chapter covers a sampling of the best and most popular backcountry areas.

The fee areas are popular both for track skiing as a sport in itself and as training areas for backcountry skiers. The groomed trails are the habitat of the serious racers, the lycra-clad ski skaters, and casual skiers who like the predictability of a marked and maintained course. Several new fee areas have opened in recent years and other areas have expanded their route systems. The commercial operators have opened up much relatively gentle terrain on private land near the roads that might otherwise not be available to skiing.

The pay-to-ski areas are highly recommended for novices since the surface is groomed, the touring centers offer equipment rentals, and the area operators provide excellent instruction. Skiers whose goal is the experience of breaking trail in the backcountry can develop the basic skills at the fee areas and then move on to the thousands of acres of skiing available at no cost on Forest Service land.

At the commercial areas you will find an operations center where tickets are sold and lessons can be scheduled. Usually there is a full-service ski shop with rentals and equipment sales either at the track or nearby. The groomed tracks are laid out as a series of loops marked with signs and flags. The routes are planned so you can ski the full circuit or you can take cutoffs that bring you back to the starting point sooner.

A snow grooming machine smooths the surface and lightly compacts the new snow. This avoids the effort of trail breaking and provides a predictable skiing surface free of the holes and soft spots that can catch a ski tip. One-way signs, designated lesson areas, and other restrictions are designed to avoid collisions between skiers of different speeds, styles and ability. The areas are usually on open flat to rolling terrain and avoid the steep tree-walled chutes that are the terror of beginning backcountry skiers in much of the Wasatch.

The descriptions for each fee area include information on the approximate length and difficulty of the track, the general setting, the services available, and directions for driving to the ski area. All the fee areas have a trail map available to customers, so this book will not attempt to list the trail details. The cost and operating hours of the commercial areas change frequently. You should call the listed phone numbers for current information.

All these services cost money and the fee areas operate as profit-making businesses. Fees are still modest compared to downhill skiing. During the 1990-91 season, daily rates for track skiing were from $3 to $10 per adult and from free to $4 for children. Season passes ranged from $60 to $130. Group instruction was about $18 per class and private instruction was about $30 per hour.

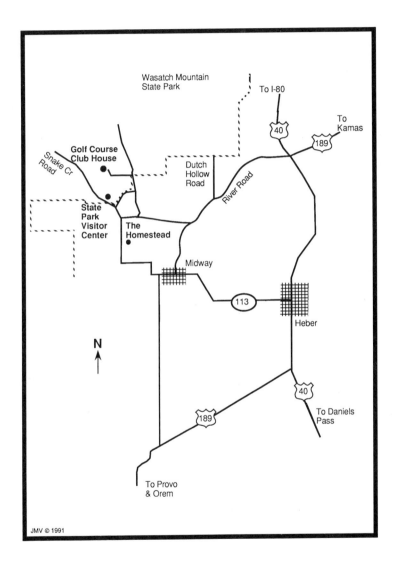

JMV © 1991

Solitude Nordic Center

Location: At the head of Big Cottonwood Canyon
Elevation: 8700 ft.
Trail Length: 11 miles (18 km)
Phone: 272-7613

The nordic center shop is near the Brighton Store on the left (east) side of the road right at the beginning of the one-way Brighton loop 15 miles up Big Cottonwood Canyon. The track is across the road. Tickets are also available at the Moonbeam ticket office at Solitude Ski Area.

This is the highest elevation of the fee ski areas and that means a long ski season from November to April and the best snow. The total trail system extends for 11 miles on Forest Service and private land on the west side of the road between Silver Lake at Brighton and the Solitude Ski Resort. The area is a mix of meadow, artificial clearings, and thick spruce-fir forest surrounded by glacier-carved peaks.

A flat track around Silver Lake, a series of maintained trails through moderate hills down toward the Redman Campground, and a steep trail that starts from the Sunrise lift are all available. There is even a short trail designed for small children. A second area of easy trails is located near the main lodge at Solitude. The Solitude Center offers instruction in classical nordic and ski skating styles on the track. It has convenient access to steep terrain and to the ski lifts and also offers instruction in telemark skiing on the hills, backcountry guide service, and avalanche classes. Solitude is an excellent training center for skiers who are starting to leave the prepared tracks and golf courses and beginning to explore the backcountry.

Jeremy Ranch

Location: North of I-80 between Summit Park and Kimball Junction.
Elevation: 6600 ft.
Trail Length: 40 miles (65 km.)
Phone: 649-2700

The Jeremy Ranch area is reached from Exit 143 on I-80 and is on the north side of the freeway. It is 8 miles northwest of Park City and 20 miles east of Salt Lake City.

Jeremy Ranch is just east of the ridge dividing Salt Lake and Summit Counties on a huge area of private land that is being rapidly developed. Besides the expensive homes and golf course, Jeremy Ranch has an extensive system of ski trails that is currently marketed as the largest maintained ski area in Utah.

They have 65 kilometers (40 miles) of trails and this includes trails that go far back into the forested hills above the golf course. Unfortunately, the low elevation and south facing slopes mean that snow conditions are often poor and the area has a short season.

White Pine Touring Center

Location: At the Park City Golf Course, just north of town.
Elevation: 6600 ft.
Trail Length: 5 1/2 miles (9 km)
Phone: 649-8701

The parking area and shop are on the west side of the main highway from Kimball Junction into the north end of Park City and are at the intersection of Utah 248 and Thaynes Canyon Drive. The Park City bus system provides local shuttle service to this area.

The Park City Golf Course was where my wife and I took our first ski lessons in Utah and despite all the recent growth it remains a delightful place to ski. The track is a serpentine path that loops back and forth over gentle hills and around small ponds. The downhill ski slopes and the condominiums provide a scenic background.

The main loop is 5 1/2 km with cutoffs to allow skiing a 3 km version back to the start. A second loop of 3 1/2 km is located across Thaynes Canyon Drive. The tracks are groomed daily.

The White Pine Touring Center provides both private and group instruction and they operate a well-stocked ski shop offering rentals and a full line of equipment and accessories. The ski area is right at the edge of town and all tourist services are available nearby.

The Homestead

Location: 700 N. Homestead Dr. in Midway
Elevation: 5800 ft.
Trail Length: 11.8 miles (19 km)
Phone: 654-1102 or 800-327-7220

The Homestead can be reached by I-80 and US 40 from Salt Lake City or from US 189 and Utah 113 from Provo. The best route coming from the north is River Road, which turns west from US 40 about 3 miles north of Heber and runs southwest along the foothills to an intersection with Burgi Lane then continues another mile west to Homestead Drive. If coming from the center of Heber, take Utah 113 west until it becomes Main Street in Midway. The main road goes through the center of town, jogs one block north, turns west for 1/2 mile, then turns north and becomes Homestead Drive. See the Midway area map.

Midway is a picturesque mixture of farmlands and fancy new homes with the Wasatch peaks in the background to the west and north. The Homestead operates an elaborate system of trails on its golf course set in rolling terrain along Snake Creek. There is a fully stocked ski shop and group and private track ski lessons are available.

The ski track is groomed and well marked with signs indicating the difficulty of each loop trail. The "easiest loop" is 1.3 kilometers (0.8 mile), the "more difficult" loop is 6.1 kilometers (3.8 miles) and the two "most difficult" loops add another 11.6 kilometers (7.2 miles) for a total of 12 miles of maintained trails. These terms are all relative and even "most difficult" groomed track is generally easier than typical backcountry skiing.

The Homestead is a long-established resort that is famous for its hot springs and restaurant. A special treat at The Homestead is a day of skiing combined with a swim in the hot pools, followed by a change of clothes and an elegant dinner.

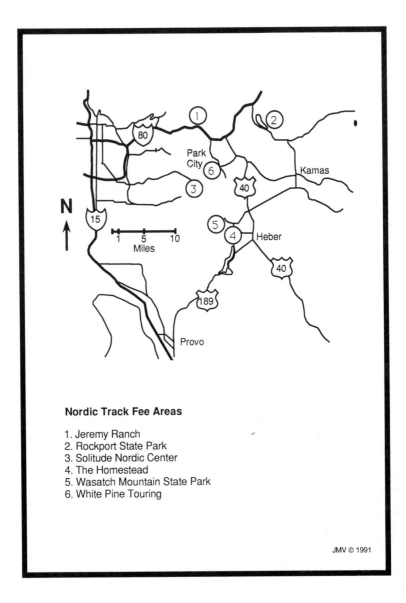

Nordic Track Fee Areas

1. Jeremy Ranch
2. Rockport State Park
3. Solitude Nordic Center
4. The Homestead
5. Wasatch Mountain State Park
6. White Pine Touring

JMV © 1991

Wasatch Mountain State Park Track

Location: On the State Park Golf Course, one mile north of Midway.
Elevation: 5800 ft.
Trail Length: 6 miles (10 km)
Phone: 654-1791

The maintained ski area in Wasatch Mountain State Park is right at the mouth of Snake Creek Canyon northwest of Midway. There are two access points where you can park and pay your fee. The main park visitor center is reached by driving north on Homestead Drive from Midway, then turning northwest on Snake Creek Road. The club house is reached by taking River Road to Burgi Lane, then turning north on Pine Creek Road.

The golf course is on the relatively flat terrain right at the mouth of Snake Creek Canyon. The ski track is separated from the adjacent designated snowmobile areas near Pine Creek Road. There is no ski instruction or rental shop at the park but full services are available a mile away at The Homestead. A small snack bar operates at the clubhouse.

The groomed ski loop is a total of 10 kilometers (6 miles) divided into a lower loop that connects the visitor center and the club house and an upper loop across Snake Creek Road.

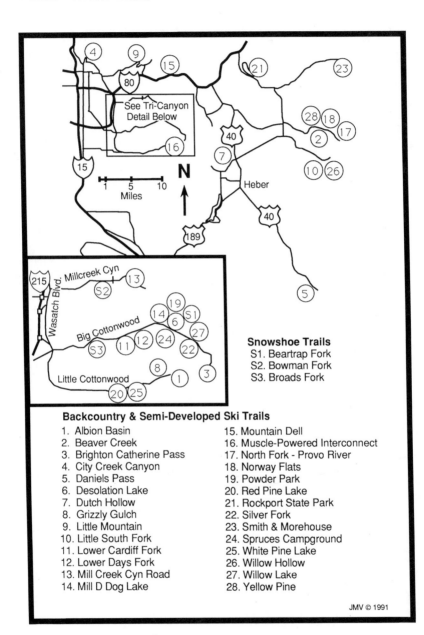

Snowshoe Trails
S1. Beartrap Fork
S2. Bowman Fork
S3. Broads Fork

Backcountry & Semi-Developed Ski Trails

1. Albion Basin
2. Beaver Creek
3. Brighton Catherine Pass
4. City Creek Canyon
5. Daniels Pass
6. Desolation Lake
7. Dutch Hollow
8. Grizzly Gulch
9. Little Mountain
10. Little South Fork
11. Lower Cardiff Fork
12. Lower Days Fork
13. Mill Creek Cyn Road
14. Mill D Dog Lake

15. Mountain Dell
16. Muscle-Powered Interconnect
17. North Fork - Provo River
18. Norway Flats
19. Powder Park
20. Red Pine Lake
21. Rockport State Park
22. Silver Fork
23. Smith & Morehouse
24. Spruces Campground
25. White Pine Lake
26. Willow Hollow
27. Willow Lake
28. Yellow Pine

JMV © 1991

6

SEMI-DEVELOPED
CROSS-COUNTRY

Rockport State Park

Location: East of Rockport Reservoir
Elevation: 6000 ft.
Trail Length: 6 miles (10 km)
Phone: 336-2241

To reach Rockport, take Exit 156 (Wanship Exit) from I-80 and drive south about 5 miles on US 189 past the reservoir, then turn east at the State Park sign. Continue on the park road, which follows the east side of the reservoir for 3 miles to the trailhead.

The entry fee to Rockport State Park is a flat rate per car rather than a "per person" fee for skiing so this groomed track is a bargain for family groups. Rockport State Park is developed around the Rockport Reservoir and is a popular boating area in summer. In winter the park is a quiet area and there are no facilities other than the rest rooms at the trailhead.

The area has 10 kilometers (6 miles) of groomed trail and consists of an easy loop through the campgrounds and an intermediate loop up Cotton Canyon. The low hills around the reservoir are important winter wildlife habitat and are an excellent viewing area.

Mountain Dell Golf Course

Location: Parleys Canyon 10 miles east of Salt Lake City
Elevation: 5600 ft.
Length: No formal route, length varies from 1 to 3 miles, generally flat.

This municipal golf course is used for skiing and sledding in the winter months. It is a fine place for the flat-ground skiing that is typical of "nordic" skiing in the midwest and it is still free-of-charge. Mountain Dell Golf Course has a fairly long season. The dynamic processes of sun and wind remove snow from hillsides faster than from flat valley-bottom areas. The golf course often has good snow remaining when the surrounding mountains are bare.

To reach Mountain Dell, drive up Parleys Canyon and take Exit 134 from I-80 (marked as East & Emigration Canyons). Turn right on the frontage road along the north side of the freeway and continue for 3/4 mile to the Mountain Dell Golf Course parking lot.

The area is heavily used and the snow is quickly packed by skiers after a storm. Some skiers make the full circuit around the golf course, which can be an energetic workout or a leisurely tour. Others use the short hills as a practice area to develop technique. The best skiing and the nicest scenery are in the narrow and wooded upper end of the area, east from the clubhouse.

A leisurely lunch stop with good friends is part of the social experience on a ski tour.

Spruces Campground, Big Cottonwood

Location: Big Cottonwood Canyon
Elevation: 7360 ft.
Length: Loops of 1 to 2 miles on flat terrain.
Phone: 524-5042 Forest Service, District Ranger Office

The Spruces Campground is a large, relatively flat area along the south side of Big Cottonwood between the Days Fork drainage and Silver Fork. The trees are thick and you are hardly aware of how close you are to the road. The skiing generally follows the campground roads on tracks packed by previous skiers. The area has long been popular with beginners and with families with small children who want a short tour. The terrain is also good for practicing a kick-and-glide style but since the track is not maintained, the serious track skiers generally go to the fee areas instead.

The skiing starts from the skier parking area 10.1 miles up Big Cottonwood Canyon. Recently, the Forest Service marked several ski trails in the Spruces area with blue signs. You can follow a short loop to the right (west) in the picnic area or a longer loop route to the left (east) through the campground or you can wander on your own. Beyond the east end of the campground there is a cabin area on private land.

Beaver Creek - Mirror Lake Highway

Location: South of the Mirror Lake Highway, east of Kamas
Length: Tours of 1 to 12 miles are possible on groomed track
with unlimited backcountry nearby.
Phone: 783-4338 Forest Service, Kamas District Ranger.

The Beaver Creek trail is a Forest Service-maintained ski route that runs parallel to the Mirror Lake Highway between Slate Creek and Pine Valley. The Mirror Lake Highway is plowed as far as the snowmobile parking area beyond Pine Valley and there are multiple trailheads along the ski trail. Beaver Creek has good access, a well-defined route and easy terrain. It is relatively level skiing through scenic country with low avalanche hazard. Those who want to do long-distance kick and glide skiing will enjoy this trail. And, best of all, it is free. All this makes Beaver Creek the recommended place for skiing by beginners who are just making the transition from track to backcountry.

The access is from the Mirror Lake Highway (Utah 150) east of Kamas. Measuring from the US 189 - Utah 150 junction in Kamas, the trailheads are at 6.1, 7.5, 8.4, 9.2, 9.5, and 10.8 miles. A large parking area is plowed on the north side across from the first trailhead. At the other access points there is either a small parking area or a wide shoulder along the road.

Main Trail

Main trail: 5 1/2 miles with 600 ft elevation gain and 100 ft descent.

The designated trail runs from the lower trailhead at Slate Creek to Pine Valley and gains only 600 feet in 4 1/2 miles before dropping 100 feet from the divide to the Provo River. The Loop Trail, the Taylor Fork trail, and the Pine Valley trail branch from the Beaver Creek trail. The route is a wide clearing through the trees and since it is a designated ATV trail in summer it is well graded. The

61

combination of occasional grooming and heavy use means that there will nearly always be a well defined and well packed track to follow. Much of the trail is in heavy aspen forest and you are visually separated from the road.

The frequent access points make many alternatives possible. You can ski in a meadow staying near an access point or you can ski the full length and back. If you have two cars available, you can do a one-way downhill tour between any pair of trailheads.

Beaver Creek Trail

Beaver Creek Loop Trail

Loop Trail: 2 miles around, 320 ft elevation gain.

The Loop Trail is easily reached from the parking area 7.5 miles from Kamas and is shown on the map. It climbs a narrow side drainage up to a large meadow, then returns to the main trail. The Mine Trail branches from the far side of the loop trail and continues higher.

Taylor Fork Trail

Taylor Fork: 1.5 miles one way, 550 ft elevation gain.

This spur trail follows a constructed summer ATV trail route up out of the Beaver Creek drainage. It climbs to an overlook on the crest of a spur ridge and offers views of the Beaver Creek valley and of Hoyt Peak. It is a chance to do some steeper skiing and gives access to the high plateau above.

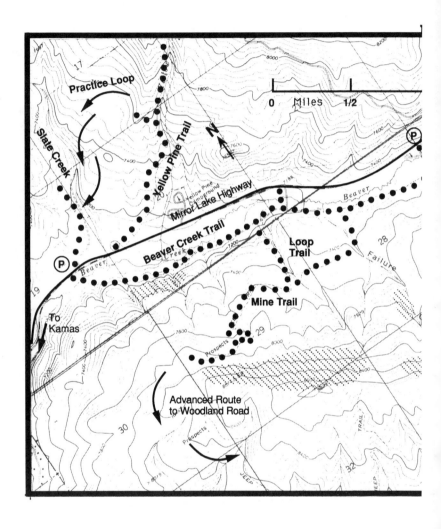

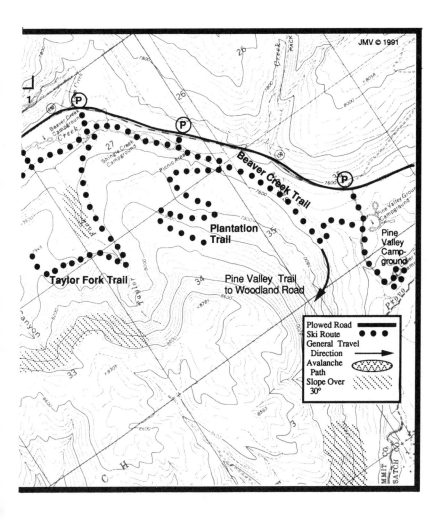

A New Year's Day tour on the Dog Lake to Catherine Pass Trail above Brighton in Big Cottonwood Canyon

7

BACKCOUNTRY SKIING

City Creek Canyon Trail

Novice tour to the antennas: 3/4 mile one way, 120 ft
elevation gain.
Water Treatment Plant: 3 1/2 miles one way, 660 ft
elevation gain.
Rotary Park: 5 1/2 miles one way 1380 ft elevation gain.

This canyon is special because it is a nature park only a
few blocks from downtown Salt Lake City. Lower City Creek
Canyon is a delightful place to ski right after a midwinter
storm. But since this is a very low-elevation area the snow
is often marginal and the ski season is short.

City Creek Canyon is reached by driving along
Bonneville Blvd., a one-way road starting at B Street and
11th Avenue. Where Bonneville Blvd. crosses the stream
and makes a hairpin turn back to the south, a short spur
road leads to the parking area in front of the canyon gate.
The ski trail starts just beyond the gate.

A ski trail has been designated along the north side of the canyon and runs parallel to the road for 3.6 miles to the water treatment plant. Signs mark where paths through the brush lead from the road to the ski trail. The trail follows a well-defined bench cut into the hillside for a water pipeline and is typically 25 to 50 feet back from the road. Skiing on the road below the water treatment plant is prohibited (a wise safety precaution since water department vehicles use the narrow road). You can continue on the unplowed road above the water treatment plant for another 2 miles up the canyon to the end at Rotary Park. The canyon is undeveloped above Rotary Park but a hiking trail leads through the brush and a very strong skier can climb all the way to the open meadows at the head of the canyon.

Little Mountain

Little Mountain Summit: 2 miles one way, 805 ft elevation gain.

The hills above Emigration Canyon were the site of some of the first developed skiing and ski jumping in Utah but the downhill skiers have long since moved south to the higher peaks. The open, rolling hills still offer excellent ski touring. There are great views of the Mountain Dell area to the east, the higher mountains to the south, and down the canyon toward the city. The elevation is lower than most backcountry touring areas and these slopes get exposed to the sun, so the best skiing is within a few days after a storm.

The rolling terrain means that avalanche hazard is low. The first time that I skied here was on a stormy day when the snow was accumulating rapidly and the tri-canyon area was far too dangerous for backcountry skiing.

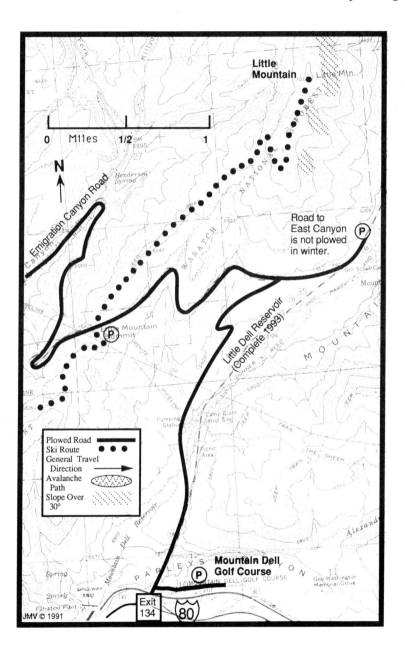

The best parking area is at the pass between Emigration and Mountain Dell Canyons, 9 miles up Emigration Canyon. Or take Exit 134 on I-80 and drive 3 miles north on Utah 65 to the junction of the Emigration Canyon and East Canyon roads then head back to the pass. The area is managed as municipal watershed and the Mountain Dell and Little Dell reservoirs are directly below, so act accordingly.

There is a lot of walking and sledding right at the parking area, but for skiers there are other nearby areas where you can play around and practice your turns. The ridges in both directions offer touring possibilities.

A good route is to ski along the ridge to the north and traverse for about 1 1/2 miles until you see an obvious way up the open slopes to the summit of Little Mountain (elev. 7032). You can also ski for a mile or so along the ridge to the south before it gets steep and brushy. The best return route from either ridge is to retrace your approach. Attempting to ski down into Emigration Canyon is not recommended due to the dense oak brush and closely-spaced homes below. Most of the higher elevation land is owned by Salt Lake City.

Millcreek Canyon

Winter gate to Elbow Fork: 1.7 miles one way, 350 ft gain.
Big Water Trailhead: 5 miles one way, 1440 ft elevation gain.
Upper Millcreek Basin: 7 miles one way, 2640 ft gain.
Wasatch Crest Ridge: 8 miles one way, 2860 ft elevation gain.

The Millcreek Canyon road is closed in winter by a gate near the Terraces Picnic Area located 4.7 miles up the canyon from the intersection of 3800 South and Wasatch Blvd. There is a parking area and turnaround plowed at the gate. The road beyond is closed to snowmobiles and is heavily used for skiing and walking. I used this road as a practice area when I was first learning to ski and still use it as a safe place to ski when there is avalanche danger on steeper slopes. It is also a delightful place for nighttime skiing by the silent light of a full moon.

Unfortunately, the heavy use means that the road becomes packed to ice within a few days after a snow storm. The glazed surface makes climbing with waxed skis tricky and makes downhill control an exercise in snowplow technique. There are no route-finding problems since you follow the canyon bottom and return the same way.

A good goal for a short tour is the Elbow Fork area where the canyon makes a sharp turn south. If the snow is good on the south-facing slopes you might try skiing a short way on the Pipeline Trail. It starts near the large boulder on the north side of the road. This trail is a bench cut into the hillside for a long-gone power plant pipeline and allows you to traverse on a level trail. This would be a perfect tour except for the difficulty in descending from the other end. The best Pipeline Trail tour is to ski a mile or so and then return to Elbow Fork.

Beyond Elbow Fork, the road continues to climb steadily to the Upper Big Water parking lot. The upper end of Millcreek is high enough to have excellent snow for most of the season and offers low-angle, rolling slopes with large

71

openings in the trees. From the Big Water parking lot you can climb the Big Water Gulch to reach the pass leading to Big Cottonwood Canyon. Or you can continue for three miles to the ridge where a pass overlooks the top of Park West's Ironhorse Lift.

This large basin is the best beginner to intermediate difficulty backcountry ski terrain remaining in the tri-canyon area. Unfortuately, the hike up the canyon road is long and few beginners are willing to suffer enough to reach this wonderful area.

Millcreek From The Top

Intermediate skiers have the alternative of ascending Mill D from Big Cottonwood Canyon, crossing the ridge and entering Millcreek from the top. This offers a shorter access to the excellent skiing in the upper bowl and uses the road for a fast glide out. The most popular approach is from Powder Park and over the east pass. Another route into Millcreek is from Dog Lake, down Big Water Gulch.

The cross-canyon tour requires leaving a car at the Millcreek gate. The ski bus can be used in the morning to get up Big Cottonwood Canyon and will drop backcountry skiers off at the Spruces area.

Powder Park Route

Big Cottonwood road to the pass: 2 3/4 miles, 1960 ft gain.
From pass to Millcreek parking area: 8 miles, 3120 ft descent.

See page 84 for a description of the route up Mill D North Fork from Big Cottonwood to Powder Park and for a map of this tour. From Powder Park, continue ascending the open, south-facing slope to reach the low point on the ridge (east of peak 9467 on the topographic maps). This is a good place to rest and evaluate the snow stability on the north-facing slopes of the descent route. The greatest danger is usually the ridge crest cornice. There are several possible places to descend. One option is to ski through openings in the trees just east of the pass, but this involves steep skiing through a known avalanche area. The easiest and safest route is to go east along the ridge until you reach the peak on the Wasatch Crest common to Millcreek, Big Cottonwood and the Park City side. Continue north a short way along the ridge, then drop into Millcreek on gentle slopes.

The terrain quickly becomes more gentle with plenty of space to practice graceful turns on wide slopes of nearly untracked snow. Simply follow the drainage downhill until the canyon begins to narrow. Here the delightful skiing ends as you are funneled into following the cleared swath of the unimproved road that runs along the stream. There are a few spots with tricky sidehill traverses but nothing an intermediate skier cannot handle, and you soon reach the unplowed road at the Big Water parking lot.

Big Water Route

Big Cottonwood road to the pass: 2 1/4 miles, 1400 ft gain.
From pass to parking area: 5 1/2 miles, 2600 ft descent.

This route is shorter than the Powder Park route but there are more trees to deal with. From Big Cottonwood, take the left branch of Mill D to Dog Lake, then continue around the north side of the lake to the pass about 200 yards beyond. This pass is the head of Big Water Gulch, which drains north.

Many route variations are possible. The best slopes are reached by traversing west across the head of Big Water Gulch. Start high on the left side of the drainage, then cross to the right side partway down. Once you are in the Big Water drainage the objective is to stay in control as you work your way down through the trees. The gulch leads directly to the Big Water parking lot where you turn onto the road for a glide back to your car.

Brighton Area

Brighton is in a north-facing bowl at the end of the road 15 miles up Big Cottonwood Canyon. The road ends at 8700 feet and the ridges above climb to over 10,000 feet. This high elevation results in a long ski season. The skiing starts from the Brighton parking lot. On popular weekends this lot fills to capacity, so consider car pooling or taking the ski bus.

Brighton was a center of backcountry skiing when the sport was first evolving in the 1930's. In recent years, operation of the groomed cross-country ski area, the resurrection of Solitude Ski Area, and lift construction by Brighton Ski Area have converted much of the best terrain to developed skiing. But the upper areas of Forest Service land still offer some good tours.

Dog Lake to Catherine Pass -Brighton Area

Dog Lake: 3/4 mile one-way, 600 ft elevation gain.
Lake Mary: 1 mile one-way, 760 ft elevation gain.
Lake Catherine: 2 miles one-way, 1200 ft elevation gain.
Catherine Pass: 2 1/4 miles one-way, 1450 ft elevation gain.

This is the most popular tour in the Brighton area and many variations are possible. The normal tour is to trudge up through the downhill ski area, climb to Dog Lake, then traverse along the ridge above Lake Martha to Lake Catherine. Beginners may want to stop near Dog Lake, intermediate skiers can easily climb as far as Catherine Pass, and advanced skiers continue along the ridges to reach powder snow below Pioneer Peak and Wolverine.

From the far (south) end of the parking lot, begin by climbing through the trees to the right of the Majestic Manor motel. The trail heads uphill just beyond the Wasatch Mountain Club lodge building and to the right of the ski lift.

Development and management changes will probably alter the start of this tour and the Forest Service plans to have a sign marking the winter trailhead. The ascent route is to climb in the trees to the west (right) of the Crest Express Chair Lift (formerly the Mary Lift). Eventually the terrain brings you out onto the downhill run. Continue up, staying near the edge and watching carefully for out-of-control downhill skiers. Climb until you see the prominent rock outcrop and the sharp turn in the downhill run coming from the top of the Majestic Lift. You will see a steep but manageable slope to the right that is usually well tracked by previous backcountry skiers. Also, there is a ski area boundary warning sign at the turn.

Get up this hill by making shallow switchbacks or even sidestepping if necessary. It is only 200 vertical feet to the Dog Lake area. Once at the top the slope levels off and the Dog Lake flats are reached by continuing southwest another 200 yards. Dog Lake is in a beautiful flat bowl with plenty of places to practice on the surrounding hills.

The main drainage is to your right and goes to the Lake Mary dam but the best ski route is to make switchbacks up the left side of the ridge above Dog Lake. This ridge takes you to a beautiful overlook above Lake Mary. From here, the route finding is tricky since you must traverse the hillside to reach Lake Catherine. If you go too high (left) you encounter steep slopes and if you go too low you will run into cliffs dropping to Lake Martha. The route crosses an avalanche path coming off Pioneer Peak. If there are no tracks to follow, you must do a bit of searching for the route that is shown on the map.

Lake Catherine is in a glaciated bowl and is a good destination for intermediate skiers. There are several avalanche areas around the head of this bowl. If you want to climb to the pass, the safest route is ski the crest of the rounded ridge running between the pass and the lake.

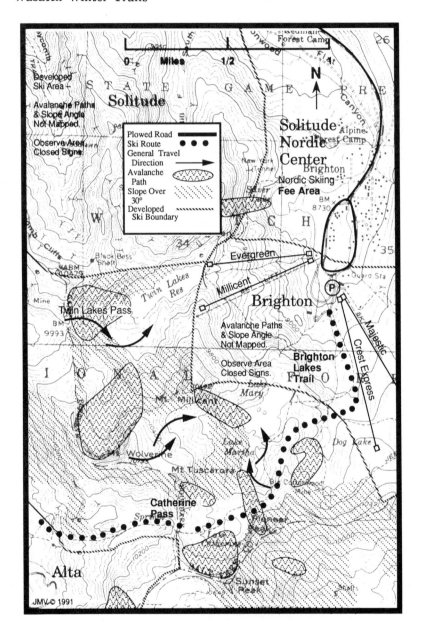

To return to Brighton, retrace your route. Descending the ridge above Lake Mary to Dog Lake and the steep hill below Dog Lake are the only tricky parts where "survival skiing" may be needed.

Brighton Lakes Variations

One popular variation is to ski along the ridge above Dog Lake, continuing past Lake Mary until you are above Lake Martha. From here you can drop down to Lake Mary while avoiding dangerous cliffs. Ski across Lake Mary to the dam, then follow the narrow drainage down to the Dog Lake area.

Another variation from Dog Lake is to ski up the right side drainage directly to the Lake Mary Dam, then explore around this scenic lake basin.

Advanced skiers enjoy the bowl on Mt. Wolverine but then must suffer as they descend through the cliffs above the lake.

Brighton to Dog Lake or Twin Lakes via Ski Lift

Using the chair lift to get up the mountain is a good way to get some skiing at high elevation without much climbing. It is good training for persons just moving from the flats to the steeper Wasatch canyon tours and introduces the skier to problems in route finding, hill climbing, and controlled descent.

Due to planned lift relocations and the ever-changing ski area policies on single ride tickets, specifics of lift-assisted routes are not described. Historically, the Mary Lift was a quick way to Dog Lake. The Evergreen Lift goes right to the Twin Lakes dam.

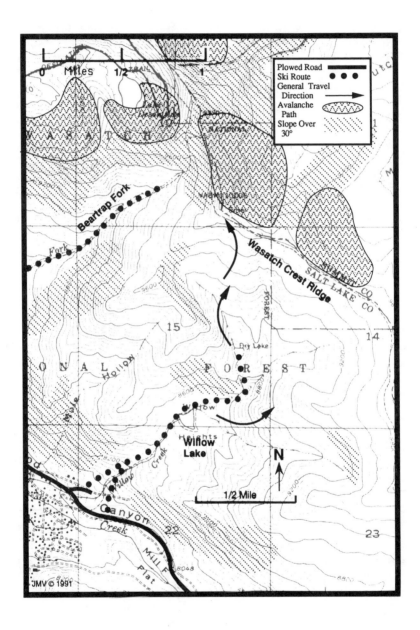

Willow Lake, Big Cottonwood Canyon

Willow Lake: 1 mile one-way, 600 ft elevation gain.
Wasatch Crest Ridge: 2 to 3 miles, 1960 ft elevation gain.

Willow Lake is on the north side of Big Cottonwood Canyon in an area of relatively low-angle terrain and open aspen forest. This is an area of mixed private, Salt Lake City, and Forest Service ownership. Respect the privacy of cabin owners.

The short tour to the lake is good for beginners. Intermediate skiers can continue past the lake and go farther up the drainage or can climb all the way to the Wasatch Crest Ridge.

Parking near the bottom of Willow Fork is a problem and you need to be creative. Fortunately, nearby Silver Fork Lodge is a ski bus stop. Observe any posted signs along the highway and around the commercial developments in Silver Fork. The summer trailhead is 12.8 miles up Big Cottonwood Canyon, about 1/8 mile beyond the built-up area of Silver Fork. Look for the Willow Creek sign on the north side of the road. An alternative is to start from the road immediately to the right of Giovanni's Restaurant. The first 200 feet of this road is plowed, then it continues as a primitive road clearing all the way to the lake.

Regardless of starting location, the best route is to follow the switchbacks of road cut on the left (west) side of the stream. Skiing is through wide-spaced aspen with good views of the opposite side of the canyon. The drainage is wide at the highway but the sidehills close in and naturally channel you to the lake. Willow Lake is in an open flat in the bottom of the drainage. The drainage forks above the lake and the ridges are fairly open. Several route extensions are easily seen from the lake.

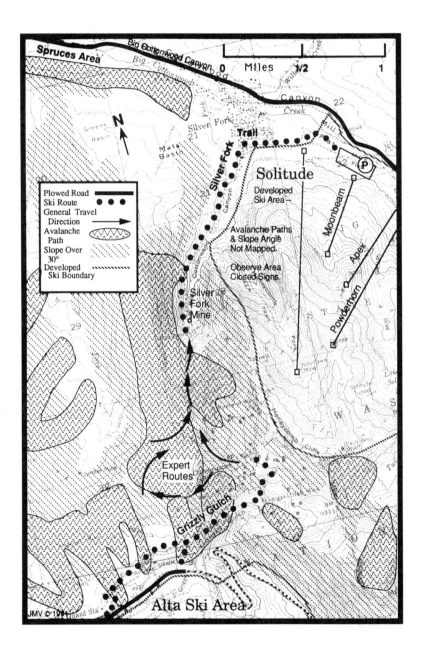

Silver Fork

Lower Mine: 2 1/4 miles one-way, 420 ft elevation gain.
Upper Bowl, East: 3 miles one-way, 1500 ft elevation gain.

The first part of the Silver Fork ski tour passes through the Solitude Ski Area, then follows the summer road along the upper end of the private cabin area and continues on Forest Service land along a closed road to the mine. The tour to the mine offers nice scenery for little elevation gain.

The tour begins at the west end of the lower Solitude parking lot 12.7 miles up Big Cottonwood Canyon. Backcountry skier parking has been permitted, but observe any posted signs along the highway and in the Solitude parking lot. To avoid crossing the downhill skier traffic, follow the blue and white signs. The signs lead you slightly downhill, behind the Inspiration Station, then along the track just below the concrete structure for the Eagle Express lift. Finally, you climb back uphill on the right of the ski runs to reach the road into Silver Fork.

Follow this road until you pass a large yellow building on your left. Just beyond this building is a road gate. Here the canyon forks and begins to narrow into a vee. The left side leads into Honeycomb Fork and you may see tracks of skiers coming down from the developed ski terrain. The backcountry Silver Fork tour continues on the road along the west side of the drainage and crosses back to the east just before the mine. The large flat area created by the mine dump is the obvious landmark.

Beyond the mine is advanced terrain. The canyon gets very steep and narrow for a way before opening up into two wide bowls.

An alternative to returning along the road is to descend the section below the mine by working your way through the trees on the east side. Look for fresh snow and easy runs back and forth. Continue down until the terrain brings you back to the road near the yellow building.

Mine shafts are a part of canyon history but are also a hazard since the openings are often bridged by snow.

The Prince of Wales Mine at the head of Silver Fork in summer. The state of Utah has an active program to close old mine shafts, especially in popular recreation areas. A reclamation crew has placed a grating over this vertical shaft. The Price of Wales shaft drops 900 feet to connect with a maze of tunnels between Silver Fork and Alta.

Spruces Parking Area

A designated parking area is located at the Spruces Campground 10.1 miles up from the mouth of Big Cottonwood Canyon. The lot is on the south side of the road and is marked by a "Skier Parking" sign. This is the parking area for Days Fork and for Mill D North Fork as well as for skiing around the campground itself. This is also a designated stop for the ski bus.

Mill D North Fork

Y-Junction: 1 1/2 miles one-way, 1010 ft elevation gain.
Dog Lake: 2 miles one-way, 1520 ft elevation gain.
Desolation Lake: 3 1/2 miles one-way, 1890 ft elevation gain.
Powder Park: 2 3/4 miles one-way, 1960 ft gain plus any runs.

Mill D is a Y-shaped drainage that has the best backcountry terrain remaining in the central Wasatch. Three beginner-to-intermediate difficulty tours and several advanced tours start from a single trailhead into this drainage.

Unfortunately, winter access is not ideal. Neither the official summer trailhead 0.8 mile downcanyon nor the traditional trailhead in the drainage near the stream is a reasonable ski route due to the south-facing slopes and the steep sidehills near the highway. The normal winter access is to take the road which goes up through the summer home area and then follows a water pipeline road to the point where the drainage widens. The summer homes are on leased land and the lots should be respected as private property. This route follows the road taking a left turn (toward the stream) at each junction until beyond the cabins.

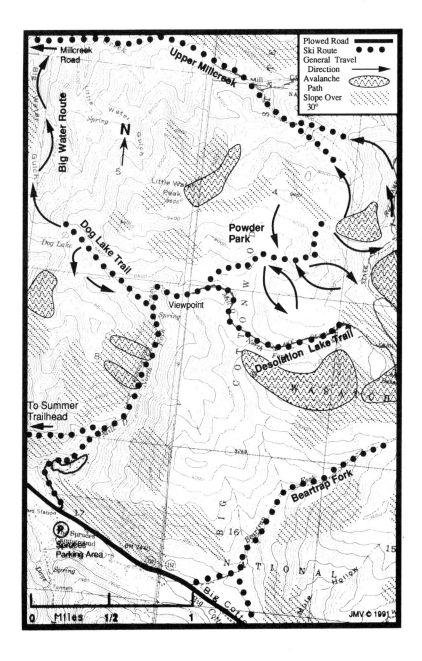

Ascending skiers follow the alignment of the summer hiking trail that crosses over to the left side and continues to climb for another mile beyond the cabins to the major fork where the Dog Lake and Desolation Lake trails separate. Along the way the trail crosses the bottom of two avalanche chutes coming off Reynolds Peak. Ski high on the opposite side if east-facing slopes are unstable.

Mill D Dog Lake

The fork in the main canyon is unmistakable. You reach a point where a steep hillside is directly ahead and there is nearly a right-angle turn to the left. In early season the top of the hiking trail sign will still be visible. To reach Dog Lake, take the left turn and head up the moderately steep and narrow chute. Take switchbacks through the trees on either side to make the ascent easier. Fortunately, it is only 500 vertical feet from the canyon fork to the lake.

Most skiers stop at the lake and have lunch. The effort of the final climb combined with the views of the surrounding peaks makes this an inviting place to rest. There is much to explore around the lake if you want to do some skiing before heading back down. The pass to Big Water Gulch and Millcreek Canyon is visible straight ahead. The upper end of the Butler Fork drainage is 1/4 mile to the west on a level traverse. The basin to the south of the lake has some good skiing on rolling terrain. Reynolds Peak and Little Water Peak rise above opposite sides of the lake. Both these summits and the spectacular bowl below Reynolds Peak are advanced routes due to the steep terrain and avalanche risk.

The descent from Dog Lake can be intimidating since the terrain funnels skiers into the drainage bottom where there is no room to turn. The trick is to ski the side hills where possible and use the unpacked snow and turns to keep your speed down. An alternative descent is to cross the low ridge immediately south of the lake into a wider drainage that parallels the ascent route. There are some trees to deal with but the slope is gentler and there is more room to turn. This drainage brings you back to the ascent route near the canyon fork.

Desolation Lake

The route to Desolation Lake is longer than the tour to Dog Lake but it is equally popular since it offers good views and has more varied terrain. To get to Desolation Lake, ski up Mill D to the Y-junction and take the right fork. The drainage leading to Desolation Lake is a hanging canyon that is entered by climbing the moderately steep slope on the north, then returning to the stream higher up. The route generally follows the alignment of the summer hiking trail but skiers usually make extra switchbacks as they ascend.

At the top of the steep hill, the trail levels off as the route returns to the stream. This is an excellent viewpoint for photographing the peaks, ridges, and canyons to the south along the divide between Big and Little Cottonwood Canyons. The route turns and follows the stream through a large meadow, then climbs into the trees beyond. Continue up the main drainage and past the tiny pond that some mistake for the lake. A last steep climb brings you over the moraine that creates a closed basin around Desolation Lake. The lake is a good destination for intermediate skiers. There is serious avalanche danger around the perimeter of the basin and nearly everyone returns by the ascent route. There have been avalanche fatalities on the ridges above the lake. Returning down Mill D, there is plenty of space in the trees to make turns and have some fun.

Powder Park

Powder Park is an area that has been discovered by more and more skiers over the last decade. The name refers to the general area north of the Desolation Lake trail where there are extensive open hillsides that are ideal backcountry skiing. Most tours in the Wasatch are destination-oriented; a long ascent to a bowl, summit, or pass is followed immediately by a fast descent. But Powder Park is such a delightful area that skiers usually take time for multiple runs down the sidehills. Most of the area is intermediate terrain with few cliffs or chutes to trap the unwary.

The first part of the approach to Powder Park follows the route to Desolation Lake as far as the first meadow in the right fork. Powder Park is the wide side drainage to the north of this meadow. The route turns north and heads into the trees on the northwest side of the meadow, then continues up the side drainage. Several route variations soon appear.

Straight ahead is the ridge separating Mill D from the upper bowl of Millcreek. Most intermediate skiers climb part way up to the ridge and ski down the wide, moderate-angle, open slope. The ascent to the ridge crest is not difficult and gives the longest downhill run. The heavily wooded north–facing ridge to the right usually has the best snow and provides great skiing through trees and small openings. The slopes to the left below Little Water Peak are another possibility, but this slope faces south and snow conditions are not always the best. Return options are to cross over into Millcreek or to return along the ascent route from Big Cottonwood.

Lower Days Fork

Lower Meadow: 1 1/2 miles, 850 ft elevation gain.
Upper Meadow (Eclipse Mine): 2 3/4 miles, 2250 ft elevation gain.

Days Fork is on the south side of Big Cottonwood Canyon and the Spruces parking area is right at the junction of Days Fork with the main canyon. This is a long canyon and the lower 2 miles are gentle and scenic, creating excellent intermediate skiing. Unfortunately, Days Fork is a hanging canyon and there is a short climb up a chute between the flat campground and the main Days Fork Canyon. Don't let this infamous chute keep you out of Days Fork.

The tour starts in the Spruces parking area located 10.1 miles up Big Cottonwood on the south side of the road. Follow the summer road that leaves from the west end of the parking lot and ski south through the picnic area toward the steep hill beyond the group sites.

The road cut makes a switchback and then enters the chute. The problem is that the chute is steep and narrow and there is limited room for maneuvering. There are no good alternatives as the hills on either side are just as steep. The bad section is only 200 vertical feet and there are several ways to handle it. Skiers using climbing skins can ascend directly up the chute using an occasional herringbone step or two. Skiers on waxed or fish-scale skis can try an aggressive pattern of sidestepping along the edge of the trail. If the snow conditions are bad, do not be embarrassed to simply take your skis off and walk up the steepest sections. Some skiers climb onto the ridge on the right that separates the chute from the stream and work their way up though the aspens on the ridge. Remember, the bad section is short and takes less than 10 minutes.

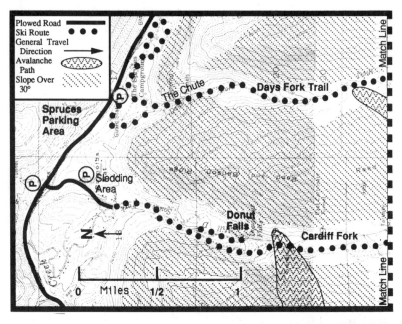

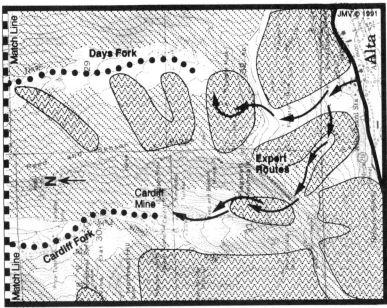

Once you are above the steep chute, the trail levels off and contours along the left side of the drainage for a way, then follows the canyon bottom. The route follows a mining-era road through alternating forest and meadows. The ascent is gradual, the hills are short, and there are nice views back toward the Reynolds Peak area. The spectacular cliffs tower above on the side ridges. A climb of 850 feet in 1 1/2 miles brings you to a good destination in a large opening near the first mine. If you have the energy to go farther, the route continues by climbing up the moderately steep hill on the right side and ascends another 1400 feet to the upper bowl of Days Fork. Beyond the upper bowl is a steep headwall on the ridge leading to Little Cottonwood Canyon. Advanced skiers regularly climb from Alta and drop into Days Fork but ascending the headwall from Days Fork is not recommended because of the long climb up slopes with high avalanche danger.

The only reasonable descent is to return down Days Fork. Rather than just skiing the ascent track, most tourers will explore variations using the more gentle side hills for variety. Near the bottom, be sure to leave the stream and get back on the main track entering the chute. When descending the chute, stay in control and watch for ascending skiers.

Lower Cardiff Fork

Donut Falls: 1 1/2 miles from highway, 300 ft elevation gain.
Cardiff Mine: 3 miles one-way, 1700 ft elevation gain.
(Will vary with location of designated skier parking)

The lower portion of Cardiff Fork offers good terrain for beginner to intermediate skiers but the quality of the experience in Cardiff Fork is affected by land status and management. The area is only partially Forest Service land. The lower part of the drainage contains a large area of private land with cabins, and the cabin owners use the road for winter access. Also this is the one drainage in the tri-canyon area that backcountry skiers must share with snowmobilers.

The bottom of Cardiff Fork is popular for sledding and tubing and the Forest Service plans call for a concessionaire-managed snowplay area at the Jordan Pines picnic area. Parking will be improved but this will involve a parking fee. In spite of the changes at the bottom, the upper part of the drainage has always been a good ski tour and should remain so.

The road into Cardiff Fork is on the south side of the main road 9.3 miles up Big Cottonwood Canyon. The tour will start from wherever the designated (and permitted) parking area is that year. The route follows the summer road past the Jordan Pines picnic area, through the cabin area, and on to the stream crossing where the road and the summer trail to Donut Falls separate.

The branch to Donut Falls is a good, level, short beginner ski tour. Be aware that avalanches have released from the steep cliffs near the falls. The other branch of the road crosses to the right side of the stream and climbs at a steady grade to the Cardiff Mine. The side ridges and the upper bowls above the Cardiff Mine are steep and have high avalanche danger so the mine is the recommended destination for intermediate skiers.

The upper part of Days Fork is popular with expert skiers who cross the ridge from Alta. You can recognize the experts by their graceful turns down the steepest slopes.

White Pine Trailhead (Lone Peak Wilderness), Little Cottonwood Canyon

The trailhead for White Pine Canyon, Red Pine Canyon, and all the drainages further west in the Lone Peak Wilderness Area is on the south side of the road 5.5 miles up Little Cottonwood Canyon. This is a popular trailhead and the parking area is often full later in the day. The trail starts near the outhouse and immediately descends to the bridge across the stream. Crossing the bridge with skis can be tricky and there is no disgrace in walking. On the other side of the stream, there is a flat area immediately to the west that is a good practice area for novices.

White Pine Canyon

Stream & Red Pine Trail Junction: 1 mile one way, 320 ft elevation gain.
Lower Meadow: 2 miles one way, 800 ft elevation gain.
White Pine Lake: 4 1/2 miles one way, 2460 ft gain.

White Pine is the largest side canyon in Little Cottonwood and provides the best beginner and intermediate ski touring in the canyon. From time to time, Snowbird has proposed expanding into White Pine and citizens have fought to maintain it in an undeveloped state. A tour up this magnificent canyon will reveal why everyone loves it.

The combined White Pine and Red Pine trail continues from the stream crossing, first south then west following the service road leading to the White Pine dam. The road climbs at a steady grade for a mile before reaching the stream coming down White Pine Canyon. Here the White Pine road turns sharply left while the trail into Red Pine Canyon turns right and crosses the stream.

The White Pine road climbs in a series of switchbacks all the way to the dam. Along the way there are good views. The ridge separating Big Cottonwood and Little Cottonwood

Canyons has fascinating geology and is very photogenic. The first large meadow, one mile beyond the junction with the Red Pine trail, is a good destination for a short tour. Just beyond this meadow is a sharp switchback which skiers sometimes miss, so watch carefully for tracks of previous skiers. The route stays on the left side of the drainage and if you are fighting through trees and boulders you probably missed a turn. Beyond the meadow you must cross the runout zone of avalanche paths coming from either side of the canyon. Higher up, the canyon opens into a wide bowl and skiers generally leave the road and go directly up toward the dam that is visible ahead. The dam and lake are at 10,000 feet and are as far as most intermediate skiers go since the slopes above are steep and have high avalanche risk.

Descend by retracing your route, but take available opportunities to ski the untracked snow on the sidehills rather than just following the road. When snow conditions are good, intermediate skiers have a wide range of alternatives to ski. Lower down, the canyon becomes steeper, and most skiers return to the road and use a strong snowplow or occasional uphill run into the powder to control speed. Fortunately, the road is not too steep and even beginners generally handle it well.

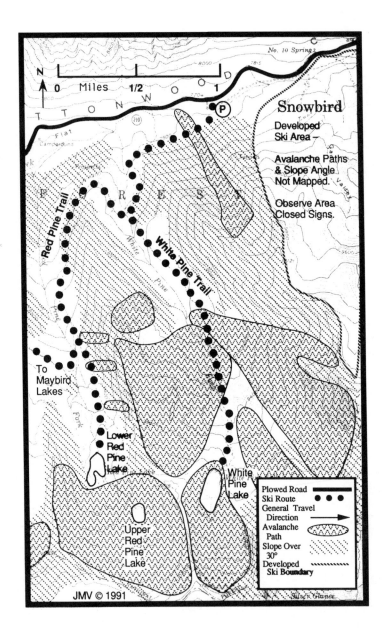

Red Pine Canyon

Stream Crossing & Trail Junction: 1 mile one way, 320 ft gain.
Little Cottonwood Overlook : 1 1/2 miles one way, 500 ft gain.
Maybird Lake Trail Junction: 2 1/2 miles one way, 1400 ft gain.
Lower Red Pine Lake: 3 miles one way, 1940 ft elevation gain.
Upper Red Pine Lake: 3 1/2 miles one way, 2300 ft gain.

This is the only ski tour described in this book that is in a designated Wilderness Area. The politics of designation in the Wasatch placed the steep rocky peaks in the three Wilderness Areas but left most of the moderate angle terrain outside.

The tour starts at the White Pine Trailhead and the first mile follows the same route as the White Pine tour. At the stream, the Red Pine trail leaves the road and turns right. There is a hiker bridge about 200 feet uphill from the trail junction but in winter the bridge is usually buried and skiers just cross the stream on snow. The trail heads generally west as it contours around the end of the ridge separating White Pine and Red Pine Canyons. The trail climbs at a moderate angle but it traverses across some very steep slopes.

Where the trail turns south and enters Red Pine Canyon there are outstanding views down Little Cottonwood Canyon. Pick out some landmarks near here so you can find the start of traverse route back out of Red Pine on your return. The trail continues climbing at a somewhat steeper grade than the White Pine trail. The route follows the line of the summer hiking trail along the left side of the drainage and starts high above the Red Pine stream. The cliffs to the left and the stream to the right converge into a narrow section near a small mine dump 1 1/2 miles beyond the stream junction. The bridge for the Maybird Lake trail crosses the stream here and is a good landmark. Beyond the narrows, some ski tourers prefer to stay left and ascend the open slopes, but the summer trail goes farther right through the trees and avoids the avalanche paths. Lower Red Pine Lake is at 9640 feet and is the normal destination for intermediate skiers. Upper Red Pine Lake is 1/2 mile beyond and 450 feet higher and is in the runout zone of several avalanche paths.

There is space for playing around and doing turns on the way down but watch for the point where the traverse back to White Pine begins. If you ski too far down Red Pine you will get into some steep, rocky areas that are not dangerous but are definitely unpleasant skiing and you will reach the bottom of Little Cottonwood at an unbridged spot far from your car.

Climbing to Twin Lakes Pass from Grizzly Gulch.

Grizzly Gulch - Little Cottonwood

Twin Lakes Pass: 1 3/4 miles, 1353 ft elevation gain.

Grizzly Gulch is a side canyon with a rich mining history. This drainage is outside the developed Alta ski boundary and leads to Twin Lakes Pass overlooking Brighton. It is also a good route to the head of Silver Fork. As you climb Grizzly Gulch, there are spectacular views down Little Cottonwood Canyon toward Mount Superior.

The easiest place to start is 8.3 miles up Little Cottonwood Canyon on the unplowed road that begins on the north side of the road right next to the Forest Service garage in Alta. The Forest Service garage is a low stone building on the north side of the highway; the Alta Lodge is across the road and a short way up the canyon. The route starts by going behind the modern wood building to the east, makes a switchback to the west behind the large grey building, then makes another switchback to the east. From here the unplowed road climbs steadily into Grizzly Gulch. Skiers who want to climb more steeply can start near the end of the upper Alta parking area and work their way directly up the hillside to intersect the road. This mining-era road gradually turns north into Grizzly Gulch and climbs at a steady grade along the left (west) side of the drainage. Be aware that the road goes below several major avalanche paths and should be avoided when risk is high on south-facing slopes.

The intermediate tour continues along the road to Twin Lakes Pass. The power line from Brighton crosses this pass and provides a landmark. You will probably notice the tracks of skiers climbing the west side of Grizzly Gulch to reach the top of Silver Fork. Partway up the gulch, there is one short but very steep section. Determined skiers can ascend this section directly but the easier route is to go to the right and make a series of switchbacks up the side slope through the trees.

The upper part of the gulch is a pleasant descent. There is plenty of room to turn and maneuver through the trees. Lower down things become more difficult. The route along the road appears much steeper and narrower on the descent. In good snow conditions this is not a problem, but if the south-facing slopes are glazed with ice "survival skiing" may be needed. Some skiers drop into the bottom of the drainage but this becomes a narrow vee-notch that is not recommended for beginners. The easiest descent is to cross over to the east (left on descent) side of the drainage high in the gulch and ski down the relatively open slopes, past the cabins, and on the Albion Basin road, which is followed down to the parking lot.

Albion Basin

Albion Campground from Alta: 2 1/2 miles, 630 foot gain.
Catherine Pass from Alta: 5 miles one way, 1500 foot gain.

Albion Basin was once the best beginner area in the Wasatch. In the past decade the Albion and Point Supreme ski lifts have converted nearly all this terrain to downhill skiing but a few pockets of snow remain for tourers who climb into the areas downhill skiers do not care to reach. Other backcountry skiers use the area for practice in developing technique on hills by riding the lifts.

Albion Basin is high above Alta at the end of Little Cottonwood Canyon. Parking is available at the end of the plowed road 8.7 miles up the canyon. The muscle-powered access to Albion Basin follows the alignment of the summer road. The road begins at the gate at the far end of the parking area and climbs in a series of switchbacks staying well to the left (east) of the ski runs. The road eventually joins the ski runs as it passes under the Albion lift. Alternatively, you can buy a ride ticket to the top.

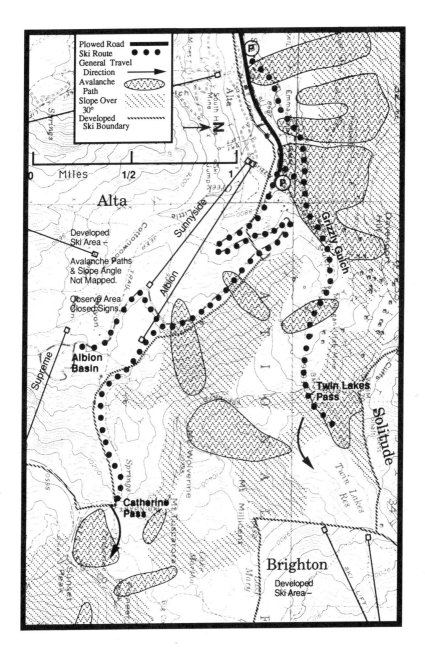

From near the top of the Albion Lift, there are two options: the campground area, or the route to Catherine Pass. By continuing to ski along the road you round the end of a hill and reach the basin where the Albion campground is located. This is open rolling terrain and there are several places to ski away from the downhill traffic.

To reach Catherine Pass, head left from the Albion Lift top station and traverse at the same elevation along a narrow trail into the upper drainage. If you go too low, cliffs will force you to descend and then reclimb a steep slope. The upper drainage leading to the pass is not heavily used by downhill skiers because of the long, flat traverse from the lift. The tour route follows the bottom of the drainage until near the top where there is a short climb through the trees to the pass. An attraction of stopping for lunch at Catherine Pass is the flock of mountain chickadees that have lived there in recent years. They have gotten used to skiers and will come around to share your lunch and will even eat from your hand.

Muscle Powered Interconnect

The much promoted "ski interconnect" already exists — at least for the backcountry skiers who have been doing these routes for decades.

One good tour is to ascend from Brighton to Catherine Pass; descend to the Albion Lift, then follow the ski run down to Alta; climb Grizzly Gulch to Twin Lakes Pass; ski down to the Twin Lakes dam, then follow the ski runs back to the Brighton parking lot. Skiing in this direction uses the best backcountry terrain for ascents and the packed ski runs for descents.

Behind The Wasatch

Most of the beginner-to-intermediate difficulty terrain in the central Wasatch has been lost to ski development but similar or better backcountry terrain can be found here on the Wasatch Back. The terrain is excellent for backcountry skiing and is readily accessible from the cities along the Wasatch Front. The drive from Salt Lake City to the western Uintas or to Daniels Pass is only a half hour more than the trip up to the top of Big Cottonwood Canyon. From Utah County, these areas are reached by driving up Provo Canyon.

The back side of the Wasatch offers huge areas with ski touring opportunities. The topography is gentler than in the tri-canyon area and this means greatly reduced avalanche danger, less energy-draining backsliding up steep slopes, and fewer terror-filled descents down narrow chutes. The selected routes are all accessible from plowed roads and are at a high enough elevation to have good snow most of the season.

This section is a sampler, not a definitive listing. There are many drainages not listed and many opportunities exist for connecting drainages by crossing the high plateaus. These routes will give a feel for the quality and variety of skiing behind the Wasatch. Once you have tried some of these routes, you will be ready to explore route variations, extensions, and nearby drainages.

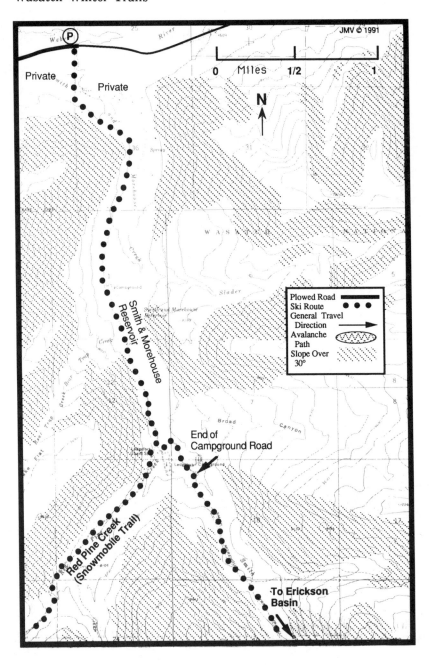

Uintas - Smith & Morehouse

Trailhead to Reservoir: 2 1/4 miles one way, 280 ft gain.
Ledgefork Guard Station: 3 1/2 miles one way, 320 ft gain.
Trail junction: 5 1/4 miles one way, 620 ft elevation gain.
Erickson Creek: 6 3/4 miles one way, 1120 ft elevation gain.

This north-facing drainage is a branch of the Weber River and is the only access through the wall of private lands along the upper Weber Canyon into the huge area of National Forest beyond. Between the Weber Canyon Road and the Mirror Lake Road are 15 miles of canyon and high plateau — definitely too much for a casual tour. The drainage bottom is gentle and would be outstanding beginner terrain except for the long distances and the serious avalanche danger from the steep side hills. A reasonable day trip is to ski a couple of miles beyond the end of the summer road and return.

Take highway US 189 to Oakley then head east on Utah 213, which follows the Weber River. Continue for 12 miles on Utah 213 and park at the end of the plowed road. The road to the Smith and Morehouse reservoir heads south just before the wood arch across the road.

The first three miles are flat skiing along the summer road, which is a snowmobile route in winter. The reservoir is very photogenic and is a good beginner destination.

Beyond the reservoir, the road continues to the campground. The road is replaced by a hiking trail up a steep and narrow canyon. To find the hiking trail, ski through the campground, keeping left until you come to a large parking lot and outhouse. There is some excellent skiing here and many opportunities for exploring. The more open side hills are worth climbing for the downhill run and you can continue as far up the drainage as your energy will allow. Strong intermediate or advanced skiers

105

can spot a car and do a one-way trip to the Mirror Lake Road.

Yellow Pine Drainage

Trailhead to end of road: 1 mile one way, 500 ft elevation gain.
Yellow Pine - Slate Creek Loop: 2 miles around, 350 ft gain.
Yellow Pine novice practice: 1/4 to 1 mile plus easy hills.

The Yellow Pine drainage is a south-facing drainage that offers the chance to explore some short tours in a backcountry setting. Near the road the Slate Creek and Yellow Pine drainages merge into a large flat that is an excellent area for novices and beginners who want to leave the groomed track and do short loop tours and practice on hills.

The Yellow Pine trailhead is on the north of the road and about 0.1 mile beyond the first Beaver Creek Trail parking 6.1 miles from Kamas.

From the trailhead, a road goes northeast toward the Yellow Pine drainage and climbs at a steady grade for 1/2 mile until it forks and soon stops. One tour would be to climb to the end of the road, continue a short way up the hiking trail which starts from the end of the left branch, and return.

A more interesting beginner tour would be to make a loop. Ski up the Yellow Pine road until the terrain gets steep, then climb left over the ridge separating Yellow Pine and Slate Creek. You will be skiing through open trees as you reach the ridge crest. You can now start working your way down the other side and return to the road following the Slate Creek drainage. This loop has some varied terrain and scenery and is a good introduction to the problems that will be encountered on longer backcountry tours.

A novice tour would be a shorter loop around the perimeter of the flat between the two drainages. The end of the ridge between Yellow Pine and Slate Creek is low angle and is a good place to practice climbing up and skiing back down.

North Fork of the Provo River

West side to overlook rock: 2 miles one way, 360 ft gain.
East side to narrows: 2 1/2 miles one way, 380 ft gain.
Meadow: 5 or 6 miles one way, 1100 ft elevation gain.
Loop between trailheads: 3 miles round trip, 220 ft gain.

The Mirror Lake highway crosses over the Provo River just beyond the upper end of the Beaver Creek trail. On the north side of the road is a delightful area of moderate skiing up a gradually ascending drainage through forest and meadow. This is an excellent place to ski a long distance without much elevation gain since the valley gains only 1000 feet in the first five miles.

There are actually two trails on the north side. The older route shown on the topographic maps is 0.1 mile west of the point where the river crosses the road. The other trailhead, marked with a Forest Service sign, is 0.1 mile east of the river. Either one offers good skiing and the two can be combined to make a loop.

A good tour on the west side is to ski along the old road clearing until it fades and then continue through the trees until the cliffs ahead and the river converge. If you continue on the west side of the river you will quickly come to a distinct gully on the left that leads upward. Near the

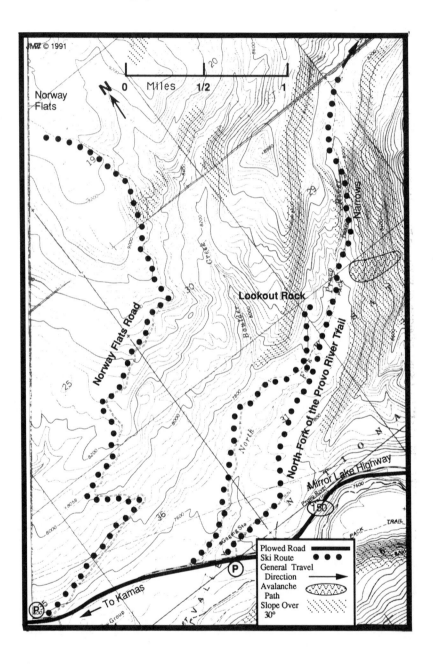

top of this gully you can turn right for a short distance to reach an outstanding overlook at the edge of a cliff overlooking the Upper Provo River. The benches along the west side of the river all slope up and end in cliffs so going much farther than the overlook is not worthwhile.

The tour on the east side follows a primitive road through the trees and over a minor ridge for about 1 1/2 miles to a parking area near the river. Beyond is a short narrows and beginners may want to turn around here. Here is where you cross the river to make a loop between the trailheads.

To continue up the east side, climb over the short hill and keep right as you ascend past a couple of large beaver ponds. The trees open up here and there are distant views of the canyon ahead.

This is the beginning of the narrows section. There is a steep slope on the right that is a potential avalanche path, so use caution if north-facing slopes have high danger. Cliffs near the river cut off travel on the left side and the side hill converges on the river from the right. At the far end of the narrows a large meadow appears on the left side of the stream and eventually the route crosses the stream (look for snow bridges) and continues up the drainage. Beyond here the canyon is wide and flat on the bottom as it continues to climb toward Haystack Peak and the high lake-dotted plateau.

Norway Flats Road

First overlook: 1 mile one way, 320 ft elevation gain.
Norway Flats: 4 miles one way, 1640 ft elevation gain.

This area is a contrast with the nearby North Fork of the Provo tour. If the north fork is too flat for your liking try Norway Flats, a misnomer since the road is steep for a long way before you reach the flats on the high plateau where the drainages originate.

The route starts by ascending the Norway Flats Road beginning from the highway across from the Pine Valley Road 10.8 miles from Kamas. The first 3/4 mile is steep and there is nowhere to ski but on the road since both sides are covered with thick oak brush. After about a mile the grade starts to ease up and your efforts are rewarded by a series of great views of the Provo River drainage and of the surrounding peaks. There start to be some opportunities to get off the road and explore the more gentle terrain to the left of the road.

The road continues climbing and after 2 miles begins to traverse a hillside before making another steep climb to the plateau above.

Willow Hollow - Wolf Creek Road

Pipeline crossing: 3/4 mile one way, 160 ft elevation gain.
Little South Fork Trail : 1 1/4 miles one way, 240 ft gain.
East fork of Willow Hollow: 3 miles one way, 1300 ft gain.
Little South Fork view point: 1 3/4 miles one way, 400 ft elevation gain and 280 ft descent with the opposite on return.

The easy access, the relatively gentle terrain, and the north-facing aspect make this the best beginner and intermediate area along the Provo River east of Woodland. The trailhead provides access to a huge area of the Uinta National Forest that climbs for 15 miles to Currant Creek Peak, far beyond the practical range for single-day ski trips. Most skiers will be content with the delightful tour up Willow Hollow or a visit to the Little South Fork viewpoint. A good beginner tour would be to continue up Willow Hollow as far as you are comfortable and then return the same way.

Take US 189 to the junction with Utah 35 in the town of Francis. Head east on Utah 35 for 10.1 miles through Woodland to the trailhead that is marked by a Forest Service sign on the south side of the road 0.2 mile beyond the end of the pavement. The ski route follows a summer road that passes between fences marking the private land on either side and then climbs up a switchback 1/4 mile from the start. Once you are above the switchback, the area to the east of the road is Forest Service land. The road continues to a turnaround where the oil pipeline crosses the route. The pipeline route is cleared and is an unmistakable landmark.

From the pipeline, a trail continues along the east (left) side of a fence for another half mile to a sign marking the Little South Fork Trail. The route follows a narrow path

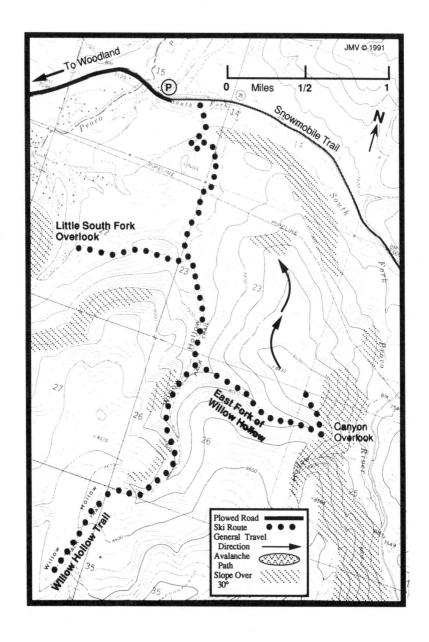

through the trees along the fence, then widens back to a road-width swath beyond the Little South Fork junction.

Willow Hollow

Willow Hollow heads southeast and climbs gently. About 3 miles from the start there is a major side drainage on the left. It is wide and U-shaped, and the bottom is a boulder field that prevents trees from filling in. This drainage climbs east at a moderate grade to a notch overlooking the South Fork of the Provo and Soapstone Mountain. An excellent intermediate tour is to climb to the top of this east fork then follow the ridge back northwest to the top of Peak 8430. From the top there are several descent possibilities. The ascent route is the easiest, but adventurous skiers can follow the ridge north and come down the pipeline route or can pick their way down through the trees until they reach the trail.

Alternatively, intermediate skiers might continue farther up the main Willow Hollow drainage, following the trail clearing which parallels the stream.

Little South Fork

Another variation from this trailhead is to go west into the Little South Fork of the Provo drainage. This is a very long V-shaped drainage and the recommended tour is a short trip to the overlook.

The Little South Fork trail starts at the far end of the ranch fence and heads back west for a mile, keeping south of the private land, then turns into the actual Little South Fork drainage. Immediately after the junction the trail starts heading up a steep hill where skiers will want to do some switchbacks. At the top of the hill there is a great view to the west followed by a more gradual traversing descent through open aspen toward the drainage ahead. The route stays high as it turns into the steep-walled Little South Fork.

The best overlook is just after turning south and before the forest changes from aspen to dense spruce-fir. Ahead, you will see the long flat valley and surrounding peaks. If you want to continue farther, the best route is to follow the summer trail clearing through the trees as the trail descends slowly toward the stream.

Willow Hollow Trailhead. The Uinta foothills have large areas of moderate angle terrain that is excellent for beginners.

Daniels Pass

Practice Flats: 1/4 to 1 mile, 100 ft elevation gain.
T-Junction: 1 1/2 miles one way, 435 ft elevation gain.
Telemark Hill (bottom): 2 3/4 miles one way, 800 ft gain.
Twin Peaks Summit: 4 miles one way, 1653 ft elevation gain.
Strawberry Peak: 5 miles one way, 1714 ft elevation gain.

The Daniels Pass area offers beginner touring up a road and over gentle terrain with minimum avalanche hazard. More experienced skiers can climb onto the ridge and ski down on moderate terrain from either the summit of Twin Peaks or from Strawberry Peak. This is an excellent backcountry ski area that deserves more attention.

Take US 40 east and continue for 18 miles beyond Heber. The start of the route is right at the summit at mile marker 36. Look for a partially buried Forest Service road sign marked "Main Canyon." Park as far off the highway as physically possible to avoid creating a hazard for vehicles or for snow removal equipment. Extended parking on the shoulder of main highways is illegal and there is a need for increased plowing of backcountry skier parking turnouts at trailheads such as this.

The tour follows the summer road which starts out going back northwest parallel to the highway for 1/4 mile and then turns west. The first half-mile is an open meadow and is an excellent area for novice practice. Beyond is a mixture of forest and meadow as you climb at a gentle grade along a minor ridge. Continue along the road past a corral, and eventually you come to a tee. The left branch is the best skiing route and you can continue for another 1 1/4 miles to reach a wide opening with the delightful slope of Telemark Hill on the left. This is a good place to stop, enjoy lunch at the edge of the trees, and then try a few turns on the open hillside before returning the way you came.

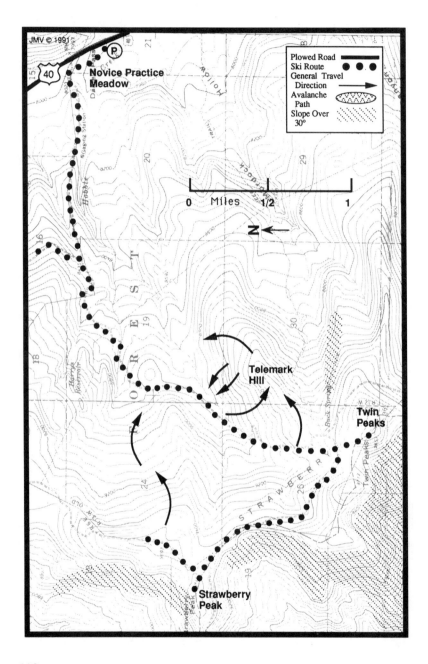

Beyond here the drainage becomes steeper and narrower, but intermediate skiers can continue to follow the road south up onto the ridge. As you near the top there are several possibilities. You can leave the road and head back northeast to reach the very top of Telemark Hill or climb to the summit of Twin Peaks overlooking Strawberry Valley. You can also follow the road northwest for a mile to reach Strawberry Peak overlooking the Wallsburg Valley. The road traverses near the top of the ridge and there are several points where you can drop from the road and work your way down through the trees to intersect the road below.

Dutch Hollow, Wasatch Mountain State Park

Skiing in the undeveloped parts of Wasatch Mountain State Park is allowed but is not actively promoted. Dutch Hollow is an example of undeveloped backcountry skiing in contrast to the maintained track on the Wasatch Mountain State Park golf course. The route goes up a small south-facing canyon.

The route starts at the far end of Dutch Canyon Drive, a gravel road heading north from River Road 2.3 miles west of the US 40 junction. The public road ends in a turnaround where two private driveways head left. The trailhead is on the right side of the road and the sign is just out of sight down in the drainage.

Ski up the bottom of the drainage through mixed forest as you follow a primitive road clearing. Beginners can follow the unplowed road grade for about 3 miles while intermediate skiers with a topographic map can continue farther and higher.

Snowshoers on the way to Willow Lake.

8

Snowshoes Only

Snowshoes are an alternative way of enjoying the winter backcountry. They are easier to master but take more energy to travel a given distance. Snowshoes offer stability and control at the price of slow speed and no thrilling downhill runs. Birdwatchers and wildlife viewers prefer snowshoes since you can stop instantly, even on a steep hill, and grab your binoculars.

Snowshoes can also be used on steep, rocky, thickly wooded trails that are difficult to impossible even for experienced skiers. Any of the backcountry ski trails listed previously can be done on snowshoes but there are plenty of destinations available to snowshoers that are seldom visited by skiers. In fact, nearly every summer hiking trail and summer bushwhacking route is a possibility for snowshoes. The only exceptions are a few, such as Stairs Gulch, that have always high avalanche danger. The trails listed here are delightful and perennially popular snowshoe tours. The Bowman and Broads Fork trails go into designated Wilderness Areas.

Bowman Trail - Millcreek Canyon

White Fir Pass: 1 1/2 miles, 1260 ft elevation gain.

The canyons on the south side of Millcreek Canyon are quite steep and heavily forested. Most of the skiing is limited to the canyon road and to experts who climb over the top of the ridge from Big Cottonwood. Snowshoes are the best way to explore these side canyons in winter and the Bowman Trail gives a pleasant climb through the fir trees with spectacular views higher up.

The trailhead is the parking area at the end of the plowed road 4.7 miles up Millcreek Canyon from Wasatch Blvd. On the south side of the main road, just below the gate, there is a road that climbs back to the west to the Terraces picnic area. At the top of the hill, stay to the right where the picnic area road forks and continue to the end. The summer hiking trail goes slightly uphill from the end of this road then traverses into the Bowman Drainage. Follow the drainage up for 3/4 mile then turn right where the trail starts climbing up the side hill. The clearing through the trees is the best landmark. Continue to White Fir Pass where you cross a minor ridge. From here, there are great views of the upper reaches of Porter Fork. You can continue up the trail beyond White Fir Pass but use caution in midwinter since there is serious avalanche danger higher up.

Broads Fork - Big Cottonwood Canyon

Stream Crossing: 1 1/4 miles one way, 1300 ft elevation gain.
Broads Fork Basin Overlook: 2 miles one way, 2200 ft
elevation gain.

Broads Fork is not popular with casual skiers. The
lower part of the route is too heavily forested and too steep to
be an enjoyable ski tour but this is no problem on
snowshoes. The route follows the summer hiking all the
way and climbs to the magnificent viewpoint on a small
hill at the lower end of the basin.

The trailhead is at the S-turn 4.5 miles up Big
Cottonwood Canyon. There is very limited parking space
and heavy traffic on the road. Usually there is space to park
on the south side at the start of the spur road or along the
highway. Take the spur road that heads south and,
immediately after crossing the bridge, look for the trail
which heads to the right past the outhouse. The trail
climbs west for a way then turns south into the Broads
Fork drainage. The trail climbs on the left side of the
stream, then crosses a bridge to climb through aspen and
meadow on the right side. There are several avalanche
paths to cross so check conditions before you go.

The trail continues climbing at an unrelenting grade to
the overlook point at the lower edge of the glaciated bowl.
Here the trail ends. Dromedary and Sunrise Peaks tower
ahead and the flanks of Twin Peaks are to the side. Travel
beyond the viewpoint is not recommended due to the high
avalanche danger.

The view of Dromedary Peak from the end of the Broads Fork Trail is spectacular but beyond there is great avalanche danger. Massive avalanches can run across the drainage and up the opposite side.

Beartrap Fork - Big Cottonwood Canyon

Upper Bowl: 1 3/4 miles one way, 1940 ft elevation gain.
Desolation Lake Overlook: 2 miles one way, 2240 ft gain.

This is another beautiful drainage where the grade is too steep and the canyon is too narrow to be a popular ski tour. The route climbs straight up the drainage and eventually reaches the ridge overlooking Desolation Lake.

This trail is between the Mill D North Fork and Willow Lake Trails. For maps, see pages 78 and 85.

The trailhead is on the north side of the road 11.3 miles up Big Cottonwood Canyon. The only parking is along the side of the road unless you walk 1.2 miles up from the Spruces parking area. The trail starts as a primitive road that makes a loop into the lower part of the fork then drops back to the highway. Where the road crosses the stream, a hiking trail continues up along the east side of the drainage. The route stays near the bottom of the drainage until the canyon begins to open at 9500 feet. From here, the open slope leads up to the pass overlooking Desolation Lake. The climb to the ridge is a long ascent and many snowshoers will choose to go only part way.

The Author is occasionally seen on snowshoes.

Phone Numbers

Utah Avalanche Forecast Center

Salt Lake Mountains
364-1581

Logan Mountains
752-4146

Provo Mountains
374-9770

Ogden Mountains
621-2362

Park City Mountains
649-2250

Business Office
524-5304

Forest Service

WASATCH NATIONAL FOREST

Salt Lake Ranger District

524-5042

Kamas Ranger District

783-4338

UINTA NATIONAL FOREST

Heber Ranger District

654-0470

Emergency Numbers

Salt Lake County Sheriff

535-5855

Summit County Sheriff

336-4461

Wasatch County Sheriff

654-1411

Other Local Guidebooks

Cache Tours by Ann Schimpf and Scott Datwyler. Wasatch Publishers, 1977. A ski touring guide to the mountains around Logan, Utah.

Hiking The Wasatch by John Veranth. Wasatch Mountain Club c/o Wasatch Publishers, 1988 (revised 1991). A hiking and natural history guide to the summer trails from City Creek Canyon to American Fork Canyon.

Wasatch Quartzite by John Gottman, forword by Harold Goodrow. Wasatch Mountain Club c/o Wasatch Publishers, 1979. A rock climbing guide to many moderate climbs and scrambles. Includes a history of the early days of climbing in the Wasatch.

Park City Trails by Raye Ringholz. Wasatch Publishers, 1984. Covers hikes and ski tours that are readily accessible from Park City, Utah.

High Uinta Trails by Mel Davis. Wasatch Publishers, 1974. Hiking, backpacking, and fishing guide to the High Uintas Wilderness Area.

These books are available in local bookstores and outdoor shops and are available by mail order from the publisher. Send for a complete list of titles and prices.

Wasatch Publishers
4460 Ashford Drive
Salt Lake City, Utah 84124

Using The Avalanche Slope Gage

For the reduced-scale maps in this book, the areas where slopes are above 30° are shaded for quick reference. All skiers should know how to check the slope angle both on maps and on the ground.

A slope gage is a handy tool for determining the angle of a mountain side from a topographic map. The entire area covered on this book is mapped on 1:24,000 scale USGS topographic maps using a 40 foot contour interval.

The gage printed on the back cover of the book gives the spacing of the 40 foot and 200 foot contour lines at angles from 20 to 50 degrees.

To determine a slope angle, place the edge of the book cover on the topographic map and match the light (40 foot) and heavy (200 foot) contour lines on the map to the pattern on the gage.

Be aware that a slope too short to appear on a topographic map can still avalanche.

Estimating slope angle on the ground takes practice. Several inclinometers suitable for backcountry use are available in ski shops. Use an inclinometer until you develop a "calibrated eyeball."

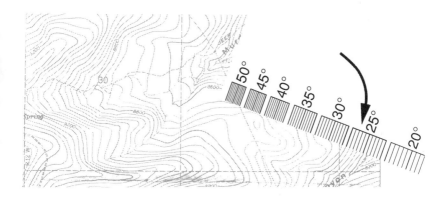

Spring Skiing at Wasatch Mountain State Park